I0456119

Fear Less

Helping Young Minds
Conquer Anxiety

By
Dr. Hannah M. Collins

Copyright 2024 Lars Meiertoberens. All rights reserved.

No part of this book may be reproduced in any form or by any electronic or mechanical means including information storage and retrieval systems, without permission in writing from the author. The only exception is by a reviewer, who may quote short excerpts in a review.

Although the author and publisher have made every effort to ensure that the information in this book was correct at press time, the author and publisher do not assume and hereby disclaim any liability to any party for any loss, damage, or disruption caused by errors or omissions, whether such errors or omissions result from negligence, accident, or any other cause.

This publication is designed to provide accurate and authoritative information with regard to the subject matter covered. It is sold with the understanding that the publisher is not engaged in rendering professional services. If legal advice or other expert assistance is required, the services of a competent professional should be sought.

The fact that an organization or website is referred to in this work as a citation and/or a potential source of further information does not mean that the author or the publisher endorses the information the organization or website may provide or recommendations it may make.

Please remember that Internet websites listed in this work may have changed or disappeared between when this work was written and when it is read.

Fear Less

Helping Young Minds
Conquer Anxiety

Table of Contents

Introduction

In a world that often seems to spin faster with every passing day, anxiety has become a common companion for many, including our youngest members. The creeping unease that can clutch us all by surprise does not spare children and adolescents, often manifesting in ways that are bewildering for both them and those who care for them. This book explores the landscape of anxiety within young minds, offering a beacon of understanding and practical guidance to illuminate the path to resilience and well-being.

Children and adolescents face a unique set of challenges as they navigate the complexities of growing up. From the pressure of academic achievements to the nuances of forming social relationships, it's no wonder that anxiety can rear its head. But, recognizing that these feelings are a part of their development is the first step towards empowering them. This book is crafted with empathy and insight, offering readers a comprehensive toolkit to support young individuals on their journey to embracing confidence over fear.

The onset of anxiety can often feel like a quietly building storm, obscuring the clear skies of childhood wonder and exploration. At the heart of understanding anxiety is the knowledge that it is not simply an overreaction or a sign of weakness. It's a complex interplay of genetic, environmental, and psychological factors. This reality underscores the importance of providing children and teens with the strategies they need to manage their anxiety, ultimately helping them to navigate life's challenges with greater assurance.

Our goal is to weave together scientific insights with emotional understanding. We'll delve into how anxiety is processed in the brain and how both inherent traits and external circumstances can trigger or exacerbate these feelings. Moreover, we'll explore how fostering open communication and emotional awareness can serve as fundamental building blocks in combating anxiety. By understanding the root causes and influences of anxiety, caregivers and young people alike can begin to dismantle its power.

Anxiety doesn't have to be a lifelong struggle. In fact, it can become a springboard for developing resilience—a crucial skill that informs how we cope with everything from daily stressors to significant life challenges. This book champions the belief that young people can learn to recognize and articulate their feelings, build emotional toolkits for handling stress, and emerge stronger from their experiences. By cultivating mindfulness and cognitive behavioral strategies, they can reshape their narratives from those defined by anxiety to those illuminated by courage and strength.

Throughout the pages, practical advice is paired with compassionate support, focusing not just on the symptoms but on the whole person. The importance of nurturing a supportive environment can't be overstated—whether it's through the formation of strong family bonds, the encouragement of open dialogues about emotions, or the establishment of safe and secure settings where children feel free to express themselves. Understanding and empathy are keystones of this process, offering young minds a sanctuary to explore their feelings without fear of judgment or dismissal.

An accessible approach to tackling anxiety also considers the modern obstacles our young ones face, such as the omnipresence of technology and social media. The potential for overwhelming pressure from these platforms necessitates a thoughtful examination of how screen time and online interactions can affect mental health. Balancing these factors with a healthy dose of offline activities, such as physical exercise and creative expression, is vital.

Transitioning into adulthood with the baggage of unresolved anxiety can be daunting. As we guide young people in building confidence and independence, it's imperative to celebrate progress along the way. Recognizing achievements, no matter how small, reinforces self-worth and motivates continued growth. The aim is to inspire not just survival of the trials of youth, but thriving beyond them—equipping young people with skills that will serve them well throughout their lives.

Lastly, this book is a call to action for caregivers. Supporting a young person through their journey with anxiety requires patience, understanding, and sometimes managing one's own stress and emotions. The role of a caregiver extends beyond merely providing; it involves being a role model and demonstrating healthy habits and mechanisms for coping with adversity. Together, young people and their caregivers can build a future where anxiety, while acknowledged, doesn't define them.

In diving into these pages, you're committing to a voyage of understanding—a deep dive into the multifaceted nature of anxiety. The insights, strategies, and stories contained herein aim to foster a space where knowledge translates into action and empathy into empowerment. Welcome to a journey that promises to transform the lives of young people, encouraging them to face their fears and emerge stronger, more confident versions of themselves.

Chapter 1:
Understanding Anxiety
in Young Minds

Anxiety in young minds can be like stormy weather, unpredictable yet undeniably real. It's important to recognize that a certain level of worry is normal for children as they navigate life's challenges. However, distinguishing between typical nervousness and more intense anxiety is crucial in fostering a supportive environment for the child. By understanding the nuances of anxiety, caregivers can better identify signs and create a nurturing space where young ones feel safe to express their fears. Empathy and patience are vital as we gently validate their experiences, empowering them to face their feelings with courage. Providing a stable foundation of trust encourages young minds to develop resilience, ultimately equipping them with the tools needed to thrive amidst life's uncertainties. Together, we can help transform anxious thoughts into opportunities for growth and confidence-building, guiding them gently towards a brighter, more assured future.

Anxiety vs. Normal Worry

Understanding the difference between anxiety and normal worry is crucial for parents, caregivers, and young people themselves. Worry is a part of life; it can be helpful, pushing us to prepare for exams or avoid risky situations. But anxiety is different. It's more intense, and it sticks around even when there's no clear reason for its existence. For young minds, recognizing this distinction is the first step in managing their emotional landscape.

Acknowledging what's considered normal worry can prevent unnecessary panic. Let's consider a child worried about starting a new school year. This worry may manifest as butterflies in the stomach or a night or two of restless sleep. It's a fleeting concern, dissipating once they've faced the unfamiliar environment and settled into a routine. Such worries are like passing clouds – they come and go, and this is perfectly natural.

Anxiety, on the other hand, is a persistent storm. It's when a child can't shake off the fear of going to school, to the point where they might refuse to leave the house or experience panic attacks at the mere thought. This anxiety isn't serving a protective role anymore; it's inhibiting their ability to engage with the world. It becomes a barrier rather than a booster, and this is where understanding must turn into action.

Imagine a teenager who worries about their grades. Healthy worry might push them to study harder and seek help when needed. But when the worry morphs into a cycle of self-doubt and fear of failure, accompanied by physical symptoms like headaches or stomachaches, it may have crossed into anxiety territory. This ongoing worry starts controlling life choices, steering them away from opportunities instead of preparing them to embrace challenges.

Now, it's important to highlight the breadth of anxiety's reach. For some young people, anxiety isn't just about specific events or situations. It can become generalized, a constant companion whispering uncertainties about everything from friendships to family dynamics. These young minds need reassurance and understanding that this isn't how life has to be – that they're not alone, and there are pathways to relief.

Yet, how can one truly differentiate between normal worry and anxiety? Observation plays a pivotal role. Frequent and intense episodes of unease, excessive avoidance of anxiety-inducing situations, and physical symptoms like rapid heartbeat or shortness of breath can all signal anxiety. Parents and caregivers are in a unique position to notice such patterns, providing the first line of support and empathy.

Empathy is not the same as enabling. It's about understanding and stepping into their shoes without giving legitimacy to unnecessary fears. It's important to offer support that acknowledges their feelings yet encourages facing fears in a safe and structured way. This empathetic approach gives young minds the foundation to build resilience and confidence in managing their emotions.

It's also helpful to realize that anxiety might not always present itself as fear. It can wear many masks – a child's unexplained anger, bedtime resistance, or sudden withdrawal from social activities could all be whispers of underlying anxiety. In these moments, open conversation becomes essential. Discussing feelings and worries openly and without judgment fosters an environment where children feel safe to express vulnerabilities.

Let's not forget that anxiety, while challenging, can serve as an opportunity for growth. It provides an avenue to teach young people about emotional intelligence, self-regulation, and coping strategies. When they understand the difference between helpful worry and debilitating anxiety, they learn to harness their emotions as tools in navigating life rather than being prisoners to them.

By learning to identify these signals early, parents, caregivers, and the young individuals themselves can work collaboratively towards strategies that mitigate anxiety's impact. They can begin creating a toolkit filled with techniques like mindfulness, deep breathing, and other forms of relaxation. Such practices empower children and adolescents to take control over their emotional health rather than feeling victimized by it.

These are not quick solutions. Anxiety doesn't vanish overnight, but with patience and persistent effort, young minds can find balance and peace. They begin to trust their inner voice, discerning when a worry deserves attention and when it's safe to let it fade into the background. Such empowerment doesn't just mitigate anxiety; it builds lifelong resilience.

Ultimately, recognizing the nuances between anxiety and normal worry equips caregivers with a clearer perspective and young individuals with confidence in their emotional journey. It's a shared mission to transform anxiety from a stumbling block into a stepping stone towards emotional well-being and growth. With this understanding, there's hope and potential for brighter, more grounded futures for young minds everywhere.

Identifying Signs of Anxiety in Children

Anxiety in children can be like an invisible shape-shifter, sometimes hiding in plain sight. Its manifestation isn't always what one might expect. Understanding these signs can not only guide parents and caregivers but also create pathways for children to voice their own experiences. Anxiety can grab hold in ways so nuanced that without a clear grasp of the indicators, it goes unnoticed, possibly leading to more significant challenges.

Children often lack the vocabulary to express the complex emotions they feel. As such, anxiety can sneak in under the radar in the guise of hyperactivity or mood swings. Some might become more clingy, expressing a need for constant reassurance or struggling with separation anxiety more than what might be considered typical for their age. Others may dive into tantrums or meltdowns when faced with unfamiliar situations.

Yet, the signs aren't always loud. Anxiety can be as subtle as a whisper. Children may become withdrawn, avoiding eye contact or shrinking back from activities they once loved. These small pullbacks can be mistaken for just shyness, but they can signal an inner turmoil. Physical symptoms are equally telling. Frequent complaints of headaches or stomachaches, especially when associated with specific situations, should not be dismissed as mere excuses to skip school or avoid chores.

A pattern of avoidance is a noteworthy red flag. If a child is consistently avoiding certain places or people, it might be due to underlying anxiety rather than simple dislike or preference. School refusal is one such example, where a child's nervousness about academic performance or peer interactions might manifest in the refusal to attend school altogether.

Sleep disruptions can also be a glaring but overlooked indicator. Anxiety can keep a child's mind racing long after their body tires. If they're regularly struggling to fall asleep, waking frequently, or experiencing nightmares, these may be signs that anxiety is at play. Such sleep issues can create a vicious cycle, as lack of rest can intensify anxiety symptoms, affecting their mood and cognitive function during the day.

For some children, perfectionism becomes a marker of anxiety. This might show in their relentless need to perform perfectly on tests or in other activities, which can lead to an unhealthy amount of stress. Observing how a child responds to mistakes or perceived failures can provide insights into their anxiety levels. If mistakes are met with severe self-criticism or the fear of being judged, anxiety may be the underlying cause.

It's crucial for caregivers to pay attention to their child's language and behaviors. Phrases like "what if" and "I can't" when recurring, may indicate worries that need addressing. Constant concerns about future events, an unwarranted imagination of worst-case scenarios, or specific fears that don't seem to fade might be pointing towards an anxiety disorder.

An anxious young mind may struggle with attention. Anxiety can lead to difficulties in focusing or completing tasks, and this isn't always due to a lack of interest or effort. The mental clutter caused by anxiety can distract a child, making it hard to concentrate, follow instructions, or retain information.

Recognizing these signs is the first step in addressing anxiety. Creating an environment where children feel comfortable expressing their worries is essential. It's about striking the balance between allowing them to express their fears and encouraging them to face them. Open communication is key, and so is listening with empathy without immediately embarking on soluion mode, which brings us to tools for managing these signs in other sections.

The journey to understanding and managing anxiety is ongoing, beginning with identifying these elusive signals. Being proactive and responsive is integral to help children navigate their feelings and find healthy coping strategies. It's about nurturing resilience and equipping our young ones with the emotional tools they need to grow and thrive amidst challenges.

Chapter 2:
The Science Behind Anxiety

Anxiety isn't just a feeling; it's a complex interplay of brain chemistry, genetics, and environment that shapes how young minds perceive and react to stressors. At its core, anxiety involves a heightened state of alertness where the brain's amygdala signals perceived threats. This reaction dates back to ancient survival mechanisms, yet today it can misfire, triggering disproportionate responses to everyday situations. Add to this the role of genetics, where inherited predispositions may tilt a child toward anxiety, and you start to see why one child's inner world becomes a tapestry of worry while another remains unfazed. The environment further layers this complexity, as experiences, family dynamics, and societal pressures contribute to the anxiety landscape. By understanding this science, parents and caregivers can demystify anxiety, turning fear into knowledge, and equipping their children to navigate their emotional terrain with resilience and clarity.

How the Brain Processes Anxiety

Anxiety is a universal human experience, and its roots lie deep within the complex networks of the brain. Understanding how the brain processes anxiety can provide a foundational knowledge that empowers caregivers and young individuals alike to face anxiety with informed strategies. At the heart of anxiety processing lies the amygdala, a small, almond-shaped cluster of nuclei located within the temporal lobes of the brain. The amygdala is often described as the brain's alarm system. It's constantly on the lookout for potential threats, helping to trigger the fight-or-flight response when danger seems imminent.

The amygdala communicates closely with the prefrontal cortex, the brain's decision-making hub. The prefrontal cortex helps evaluate and moderate the response triggered by the amygdala. When functioning optimally, this partnership ensures that we respond appropriately to our environment. However, in individuals prone to anxiety, particularly in developing brains, the amygdala can go into overdrive, perceiving threats where there may be none or amplifying minor stressors into overwhelming ones. This imbalance can lead to the characteristic symptoms of anxiety, such as restlessness, rapid heartbeat, and an overpowering sense of worry.

In children and adolescents, the prefrontal cortex is still maturing. This means that their ability to regulate the emotional responses triggered by the amygdala is not yet fully developed. When anxiety strikes, young individuals may find it challenging to apply reason and logic to their emotional reactions. But here's the inspiring part: the brain is adaptable. With time and the right strategies, young people's brains can learn to achieve a better balance between emotion and reasoning, reducing the intensity of anxious responses.

The hippocampus also plays a crucial role in anxiety. This part of the brain is involved in forming, organizing, and storing memories, and it has a significant impact on our emotional responses. Experiences of anxiety can be stored as memories, and in future similar situations, these can be reactivated, triggering the amygdala. Understanding this process underscores the importance of addressing anxiety early. By equipping young minds with tools and strategies that promote healthy memory processing, we can mitigate the reinforcement of anxious responses.

Neurotransmitters, the chemical messengers of the brain, are also involved in how the brain processes anxiety. GABA (gamma-aminobutyric acid), serotonin, and norepinephrine are key players here. GABA is the brain's primary inhibitory neurotransmitter, playing a role in reducing neuronal excitability throughout the nervous system. A deficiency in GABA activity is often associated with increased anxiety. Serotonin influences mood, and low levels are commonly linked to anxiety and depression. Norepinephrine, on the other hand, is involved in responses to stress and panic. The balance and interaction of these chemicals can significantly influence an individual's experience of anxiety.

During adolescence, the brain undergoes a myriad of changes as it shapes itself into adult form. These changes can exacerbate feelings of anxiety. The brain's plasticity during this period is both an opportunity and a challenge. It means that the brain is highly receptive to learning and adaptation, which is beneficial for adopting new coping strategies. However, it also means that adolescents may be particularly sensitive to stressors due to the ongoing development of brain circuits.

It's essential to differentiate between helpful anxiety, which drives us to meet deadlines and prepare for challenges, and the unhelpful anxiety that hinders daily functioning. Helpful anxiety is the brain's way of ensuring we're alert and prepared for important tasks or danger. It's the body's natural response to perceived threats, mobilizing energy and focus. Yet when the system is hyperactive — when the amygdala triggers too frequently without real cause — it becomes unhelpful, leading to chronic anxiety.

Research in neuroscience provides hope through the concept of neuroplasticity. The brain has the ability to rewire its connections throughout life. Mindfulness practices, cognitive behavioral techniques, and therapies designed to target anxiety can all contribute to reshaping neural pathways. By integrating these practices into daily routines, children and adolescents can begin to build resilience against anxiety, effectively training their brains to respond differently to stressors.

In conclusion, by understanding the biological underpinnings of anxiety, we can demystify the experience and approach it with compassion and practicality. Recognizing that the brain's natural wiring significantly influences anxiety lands us in a position of empowerment. With the right support, both at home and within educational frameworks, young individuals can learn to navigate their brain's responses more effectively. This understanding is the first step towards utilizing strategies and tools that promote mental well-being, fostering a future where anxiety does not define them but rather becomes just one aspect of their rich and varied human experience.

Role of Genetics and Environment

Anxiety in young people isn't just a byproduct of their experiences; it's also woven into the fabric of their very being through the interplay of genetics and environment. Understanding this intricate dance helps parents and caregivers pinpoint how anxiety can originate and manifest in their children, paving the way for more personalized strategies to support them.

The role of genetics in anxiety is a reminder that biology significantly influences our feelings and behaviors. Research has shown that anxiety-related traits can indeed run in families. If a child's family history includes anxiety disorders, there's a higher likelihood that the child might experience similar challenges. This doesn't mean that anxiety is an unavoidable fate, but rather that there's a predisposition that can be influenced and moderated through understanding and intervention.

Genetic factors involve various genes that interact with each other in complex ways, affecting brain function. These genes can influence neurotransmitter systems, like serotonin and dopamine, which play crucial roles in mood regulation and stress response. Children born with genetic vulnerabilities may have a more sensitive amygdala, the brain's fear center, making them more susceptible to anxiety when faced with stress.

But let's not underestimate the power of environment. While genetics may load the gun, the environment pulls the trigger. A child's surroundings – family dynamics, social interactions, and life events – significantly shape how anxiety develops and is expressed. On one hand, nurturing environments with supportive relationships can buffer against genetic predispositions. On the other, environments marked by stress, unpredictability, or trauma can amplify anxiety symptoms, particularly in those with genetic vulnerabilities.

There is substantial evidence showing that environmental factors like parenting styles contribute to the onset and persistence of anxiety. For instance, overprotective parenting may inadvertently reinforce a child's perception of the world as unsafe, fueling anxiety. Conversely, environments that encourage independence and problem-solving can promote resilience, even in genetically predisposed children.

School settings play a pivotal role, too. Academic pressures, social hierarchies, and bullying are environmental stressors that can trigger or worsen anxiety. A child predisposed to anxiety may find these challenges particularly daunting, making school a significant arena for intervention. Schools that foster inclusive communities and encourage emotional expression can mitigate environmental stressors.

Moreover, the current era's technology-driven world introduces new environmental variables. Constant exposure to social media can amplify anxiety, especially in youth who already have a genetic tendency toward anxiety disorders. The environment extends even to the digital spaces young people inhabit, where idealized portrayals of life and cyberbullying can create overwhelming pressures.

It's crucial to acknowledge that it's not just negative environmental factors at play. Positive interventions can significantly alter a child's trajectory. Building robust family bonds, affirming friendships, and creating consistent routines can provide a sense of stability and security. Mindfulness practices and open conversations about emotions are environmental strategies that help mitigate anxiety.

Imagine this: a garden with seeds that carry the potential for beautiful blossoms but also weeds. Genetics provides the seeds, including some that may predispose a child to anxiety. The environment is the soil, sunlight, and water that determine which seeds grow and how they flourish. By cultivating a nourishing environment, we can promote healthy development and resilience, even when the seeds carry vulnerabilities.

So, what can parents and caregivers do? First, they can embrace a deeper understanding of their child's unique genetic makeup and environment. Creating an open dialogue about family history of mental health can demystify genetics, offering parents insight into patterns that may emerge. Parents should take heart in knowing that their actions can profoundly impact how genetic predispositions play out.

Practically, families can work to create environments that foster emotional security and resilience. Encouraging autonomy, listening without judgment, and modeling positive relationship skills are foundational steps. In addition, balancing school and social life pressures with leisure and play helps young people navigate their path.

Ultimately, the interplay of genetics and environment in anxiety isn't simply a scientific fact to be noted. It is a dynamic element of human experience. By acknowledging the influence of both nature and nurture, parents and caregivers equip themselves with the knowledge to guide their children more effectively. Through supportive environments, the adverse effects of genetic predispositions can be tempered, fostering a future where confidence and resilience bloom.

Chapter 3:
Building an Emotional Toolkit

In the whirlwind of growing up, emotions can often feel unpredictable and overwhelming, especially for young ones grappling with anxiety. Building an emotional toolkit is about equipping children and adolescents with the essential tools to recognize and articulate their feelings, transforming emotional chaos into comprehensible experiences. By identifying and naming their emotions, young people can begin to understand their inner world, paving the way for effective self-regulation and healthy coping strategies. It's about seeing emotions not as hurdles, but as stepping stones toward resilience. Imagine a child learning to calm their racing heart through deep breaths or a teen choosing to journal rather than withdraw during tough times. These practices, simple yet profound, empower them to navigate life's ebbs and flows with greater confidence and adaptability. As we guide them on this journey, we foster an environment where they feel supported and understood, teaching them that it's not just about handling anxiety; it's about embracing their potential to thrive despite it.

Recognizing Feelings

Understanding and recognizing feelings is the cornerstone of building an emotional toolkit that equips young people to navigate anxiety with resilience and confidence. Feelings are complex, often bubbling beneath the surface, making them difficult for children and adolescents to identify and articulate. However, this key skill lays the foundation for effective emotional regulation and coping strategies. It starts with teaching young people to tune into their internal worlds and acknowledge what they feel without judgment or shame.

Children often struggle with naming their emotions because they haven't had the experience to make those distinctions yet. Confusion can arise as feelings can overlap or happen simultaneously, leading to misunderstandings about their emotional states. As caregivers and mentors, it is crucial to guide young people in becoming emotionally literate. This doesn't just involve naming emotions like sadness, anger, or joy. It means helping them understand the nuances, such as frustration versus anger or excitement versus anxiety.

Introducing the concept of the emotional spectrum can be incredibly beneficial. Think of emotions as colors; just as there are countless shades of blue, there are countless variations of joy, fear, and everything in between. By expanding their emotional vocabulary, children and adolescents can begin to express what they are experiencing in more precise terms. This clarity can reduce anxiety as they make sense of their emotional turmoil and feel more in control.

The journey toward emotional literacy can be as direct as creating regular opportunities for emotional check-ins. Ask questions like, "What are you feeling right now?" or "Can you describe this feeling in the shape or color it might have?". This simple practice can encourage introspection and frequent reflection, allowing children to recognize patterns in their emotional responses. Over time, this helps them prepare better for similar situations in the future.

It's also essential to validate feelings, regardless of whether they seem rational or not. Many adults unintentionally dismiss children's feelings by saying things like, "There's nothing to be afraid of" or "Big kids don't cry." While these statements are often meant to console, they can inadvertently discourage kids from sharing what they truly feel. Instead, we should aim to listen actively and respond with empathy, affirming their right to feel as they do. Reassuring statements such as "It's okay to feel scared; let's talk about why you might be feeling this way" can make a significant difference.

Consider feelings as natural responses to the world, like a compass guiding actions and decisions. When kids understand that feelings are not weaknesses but powerful indicators of their needs and desires, they can be more accepting of themselves. This acceptance is crucial in reducing the stigma that often surrounds anxiety and emotional expression.

Moreover, caregivers can model emotional intelligence by openly discussing their own feelings in a responsible way. Sharing personal experiences like, "I felt overwhelmed at work today, and here's how I handled it," provides real-life context and exemplifies healthy emotional management. Demonstrating vulnerability can teach young people that they are not alone in their experiences, and talking about feelings is a healthy, normal part of life.

Interactive activities can also enhance emotional recognition. Drawing, painting, or writing stories encourage children to explore their emotions creatively. When young people engage in such artistic expressions, they often access emotions that they couldn't put into words. These mediums can bridge the gap between feeling and understanding.

Incorporating play is another effective method. Games that focus on emotions—such as role-playing different scenarios or using flashcards that depict diverse emotional faces—can make learning about emotions engaging and less daunting. Through play, children experiment with feelings in a safe environment and learn to identify and name them accurately.

Incorporating mindfulness into daily routines can also promote emotional awareness. Mindful practices like body scans or focused breathing teach young people to tune into their physical sensations, which are often the first indicators of emotions in the body. Over time, children can develop an acute awareness of how different emotions manifest within them, allowing for earlier intervention and better management of anxiety.

Recognizing feelings is not a skill children acquire overnight; it's an ongoing journey that evolves with time and experience. The more that young people learn to recognize their feelings, the better equipped they'll be to tackle anxiety and other challenges. They build an essential skillset that carries into adulthood, helping them face life's pressures with emotional resilience and confidence.

Developing Healthy Coping Strategies

In the journey of constructing a robust emotional toolkit, learning to develop healthy coping strategies plays a pivotal role. It's akin to furnishing a toolbox with varied and adaptable tools, ready to address the unique challenges young people face as they navigate their worlds. These strategies are not merely tricks or quick fixes; they are cultivated habits and practices that empower children and adolescents to manage their anxiety effectively.

Coping strategies are diverse, just as the sources of anxiety are. Recognizing that each child and adolescent has individual needs and responses is key. So, it's crucial to help them identify what works best for them in their circumstances. Coping strategies might include physical activities like running or yoga, creative outlets such as drawing or writing, or cognitive approaches like reframing negative thoughts. The variety allows for flexibility and experimentation, encouraging young people to tailor strategies to fit their personal experiences and preferences.

Consider, for instance, the profound impact of physical exercise. Exercise isn't just about keeping the body healthy; it's a vital tool for mental health as well. When engaging in physical activity, the body releases endorphins, naturally occurring chemicals in the brain that enhance mood and promote a sense of well-being. These are often likened to natural anti-anxiety agents, and regular physical activity can significantly reduce stress levels. Encouraging children and adolescents to integrate such activities into their routines can be transformative, not just in combating anxiety but in bolstering overall resilience.

Creative expression offers another powerful outlet for managing anxiety. Art, music, and writing provide a safe space for emotions to be explored and expressed, often revealing hidden anxieties that might not be readily verbalized. For example, drawing or painting can serve as a form of meditation, quieting racing thoughts and offering a tangible focus. Journaling, too, is an introspective practice that allows young people to articulate their feelings, leading to insights and emotional clarity. These creative pursuits serve as both an escape and a way to process complex emotions, reinforcing an internal dialogue that is compassionate and understanding.

Moreover, teaching cognitive strategies provides young people with a means to navigate their thoughts and emotions constructively. Cognitive techniques such as cognitive restructuring help in challenging and altering distorted or negative thinking patterns. By guiding children to question the accuracy of their anxious thoughts and encouraging them to replace them with more balanced ones, we build their capacity to approach anxiety with curiosity rather than fear. It's a shift from "Why am I feeling this way?" to "What can I do about it?" This empowered perspective reinforces a problem-solving mindset, underscoring that while they may not control every situation they face, they can control how they respond to it.

Cultivating mindfulness practices complements these strategies by encouraging present-moment awareness. Mindfulness helps in managing anxiety by redirecting the focus from overwhelming future possibilities or distressing past experiences to the present moment. Techniques such as mindful breathing or counting practices can anchor young people in the now, reducing the intensity of anxious feelings. It emphasizes non-judgmental self-awareness, allowing them to gently observe their emotions without immediate reaction. This creates a buffer, providing a calming space to identify and choose appropriate coping responses.

As we guide young ones in building these skills, it's vital to remember the role of environment and support. Caregivers and educators should foster spaces that validate and encourage these coping mechanisms. Practicing these strategies doesn't happen in isolation; consistent support and positive reinforcement from trusted adults are crucial. Encouraging young people by celebrating small victories and progress fosters a growth mindset. It ensures they perceive their coping efforts not as chores but as empowering choices that shape their emotional landscape.

It's also helpful to instill the understanding that developing healthy coping strategies takes time and patience. It's not about finding an immediate solution but about building resilience over time. Effective coping doesn't mean anxiety will never occur; rather, it's about handling anxiety more constructively. The process is akin to planting a garden that requires nurturing and patience, knowing it will flourish with care. This perspective encourages persistence and reduces feelings of frustration when progress isn't immediately apparent.

In initiating this development, one can start with discussions around recognizing triggers and understanding the body's response to stress. By demystifying anxiety and breaking it down into understandable parts, children and adolescents can feel more in control. Identifying what triggers their anxiety is the first step toward mitigating its effects. Once those triggers are identified, personalized coping strategies can be effectively implemented, turning potential anxiety-inducing situations into opportunities for practice and growth.

Finally, empowering young people with healthy coping strategies is about encouraging agency. It's a process of teaching them to fish, rather than simply giving them fish. Through practicing these strategies and experiencing their benefits, they not only learn how to cope with immediate challenges but also how to build a foundation for lifelong emotional well-being. They develop confidence, knowing they have a toolkit of resources to draw upon whenever faced with adversity. This sense of preparedness can offer remarkable peace of mind, speaking volumes to the resilience that lies within each young individual.

In essence, developing healthy coping strategies is central to nurturing a child's ability to handle anxiety both now and in the future. By equipping them with these tools, we empower young people to navigate the ups and downs of life with greater assurance and self-awareness. This empowerment leads not only to reduced anxiety in the moment but fosters a broader sense of confidence and competence, serving as a cornerstone for building deep-rooted resilience.

Chapter 4:
Communicating About Anxiety

Open conversations about anxiety might seem daunting, yet they're crucial stepping stones towards healing and understanding. It's all about creating a dialogue where children feel safe and supported to share their worries without fear of judgment. Encouraging your child to express their feelings in a space where listening ears are attentive—without jumping to resolve the discomfort—is key to helping them navigate anxiety's turbulent waters. Rather than offering solutions immediately, try empathizing and validating their emotions, fostering trust and comfort. By showing patience and curiosity, you empower young minds to articulate their experiences, transforming silent struggles into shared journeys. This ongoing, empathetic communication not only builds resilience but also lays the groundwork for a lifelong skill set in managing stress and adversity, ensuring they're never alone in their battle against anxiety.

Encouraging Open Conversations

Open conversations about anxiety can create a sense of trust and understanding that is crucial for helping young people navigate their emotions. It's important to foster an environment where kids feel comfortable expressing their feelings without fearing judgment or dismissal. This doesn't mean you need to have all the answers. Sometimes, simply listening and acknowledging their experiences can be incredibly powerful.

The first step in encouraging these conversations is to create a safe space. When children or teens talk about their anxiety, they can be incredibly vulnerable. Demonstrating empathy and reassuring them that their feelings are valid establishes a foundation of trust. Remember, your role isn't to fix or solve their problems immediately, but to offer support and understanding. This encourages them to open up and discuss their emotions freely, which can be incredibly liberating.

In homes where conversations about emotions are already ongoing, adding discussions about anxiety might be easier. However, in families where these topics aren't commonly discussed, initiating this dialogue can seem daunting. To ease into it, look for natural opportunities to talk—perhaps during car rides, when the pressure of face-to-face interaction is less intense, or during walks. The goal is to make these discussions feel casual and unforced, part of everyday life rather than something to be undertaken sporadically.

Sometimes, asking open-ended questions can be helpful. For example, instead of asking, "Are you feeling anxious?" which demands a yes or no answer, try, "What's been on your mind lately?" or "How do you feel about that?" These questions invite more detailed responses and encourage your child to explore their feelings more deeply.

It's also essential to model the behavior you want to see. If you share your experiences with anxiety or stress (in an age-appropriate way), it sends a message that these conversations are okay to have. Children learn a lot through observation, and when they see adults honestly discussing emotions, they're more likely to do the same. This helps demystify anxiety and reduces any stigma associated with feeling nervous or overwhelmed.

Emphasize active listening during these conversations. Show you're engaged by nodding, maintaining eye contact, and reflecting back what they're saying. Phrases like, "That sounds really tough" or "I can see why that would make you anxious" can validate their feelings and encourage further dialogue. Try to put aside any distractions, like phones or televisions, and give your full attention.

However, sometimes, despite the best intentions, children might still be reluctant to talk. It's important to recognize that this is normal, and pushing them too hard can be counterproductive. Be patient and let them know you're there when they're ready to chat. You can leave small openings in the conversation for them to fill in when they feel comfortable.

Creating a regular routine around checking in can also be beneficial. Whether it's a weekly family meeting, a nightly bedtime chat, or another consistent time, having a set schedule can give children something to count on. Regular check-ins can make conversations about anxiety a norm rather than an exception, further normalizing these discussions.

While encouraging open conversations, be mindful of the language you use. Avoid phrases that could unintentionally belittle or dismiss their feelings, such as "You'll be fine," or "You're overreacting." These can shut down communication and prevent them from coming to you in the future. Instead, expressions of empathy and support, like "I'm here for you," or "I understand how you might feel," can open doors to meaningful conversations.

Utilizing tools like visual aids or mood tracking apps can also help open lines of communication. Visual aids, such as emotional color wheels, can help children identify and articulate their feelings. Similarly, mood-tracking apps allow them to record their feelings over time, and reviewing this data together can serve as a discussion starter that may highlight patterns or triggers you can work on together.

Another strategy is to integrate educational resources, such as books or videos about anxiety, into your discussions. These resources can explain concepts in relatable ways and provide a shared basis for talking through difficult topics. They serve as neutral ground that can make discussing personal experiences less intimidating.

Encouraging open conversations isn't just about focusing on anxiety, but also about celebrating successes and positive moments. Don't forget to talk about what goes well, what makes them happy, and what they're proud of. This not only balances the conversation but also reinforces resilience and builds confidence.

In fostering open conversations, remember it's a journey that takes time, patience, and a lot of encouragement. Sometimes you'll make mistakes, and that's okay. The key is to stay committed to the process and open to learning along with your child. Your willingness to engage in these conversations speaks volumes and demonstrates that anxiety is something that can be managed together, as a team.

As these conversations unfold, young individuals will likely feel more empowered to face their fears and challenges. Over time, this open dialogue can help them develop coping strategies, build resilience, and gain a deeper understanding of themselves. Ultimately, the goal is to equip them with the tools to navigate their world with confidence and ease, knowing they have your unwavering support every step of the way.

Listening Without Judgment

Effective communication is the cornerstone of understanding and managing anxiety, especially in young people. Listening without judgment forms the basis of such communication. It's not always about offering solutions or advice. It's about creating a safe environment where feelings and thoughts can be shared openly.

Imagine the difference it makes when a child knows they can express their worries without fear of criticism. Listening without judgment is not something that happens naturally for everyone. It's a skill that takes time and effort to develop. By focusing on what a young person is saying rather than how it makes you feel, you're already taking the first few steps toward empathetic listening. This act alone can make a profound impact on their emotional well-being.

The process of listening goes beyond simply hearing the words being spoken. It's about picking up on non-verbal cues such as tone of voice, body language, and even silence. Sometimes what isn't said can be just as revealing as what is spoken. These cues can provide insight into the depth of a child's feelings and can guide you on how to offer the most effective support.

An effective listener uses verbal affirmations to encourage the speaker. Simple phrases like "I understand," "Tell me more," or "That must be hard" are more supportive than you might initially think. These affirmations convey empathy and understanding, encouraging the child to continue sharing.

When listening to a young person talk about anxiety, avoid interrupting with solutions or reassurances that might downplay their feelings. Statements like "Don't worry" or "It's not a big deal" might seem comforting, but they can inadvertently dismiss what the child is experiencing. This can lead to feelings of isolation, making it harder for the child to open up in the future.

It's natural to want to ease a young person's distress, especially if you're a parent or caregiver. However, by allowing them to express their emotions fully, you empower them to identify their own feelings. This, in turn, helps them to develop better emotional awareness and resilience. Listening without judgment, therefore, plays a dual role in both comforting the child and fostering their emotional growth.

Consider using open-ended questions to engage deeper dialogue. Instead of asking, "Are you worried about the test?" you might say,

"What are your thoughts about the test coming up?" This approach gives children the space to explore their feelings openly. It also minimizes the risk of putting words in their mouth or swaying their thoughts toward any preconceptions you might have.

Maintaining a comforting presence also involves managing your own reactions. Your facial expressions, tone of voice, and body language can speak volumes. Something as simple as maintaining eye contact and nodding affirmatively while they talk can reassure the child that they are being heard and valued. Even a gentle, understanding touch on the shoulder can go a long way in showing support.

If a child expresses feelings that shock or upset you, it's crucial to remain calm and collected. Responding with alarm or disbelief can shut down an open conversation faster than anything. Remind yourself that your primary role here is to listen and comprehend, not to judge or react defensively.

Reflective listening can also be a powerful tool. By paraphrasing what the child has said, you show that you're following their narrative closely. It gives the opportunity to clarify any misunderstandings and validate their feelings. For instance, saying, "It sounds like you're feeling quite overwhelmed about school because..." allows them to confirm or elaborate on their thoughts.

When these techniques are put into practice consistently, they'll help establish a communication pattern that young minds will find reassuring. They will learn to trust you with their thoughts and feelings, secure in the knowledge that they will be met with compassion, not criticism.

Remember, fostering such open lines of communication is an ongoing process, not a one-time effort. Over time, the consistent practice of listening without judgment can transform the way young people experience and understand their anxiety. They'll be more likely to explore their feelings and learn self-reflection, leading to a deeper emotional resilience that can help manage anxious thoughts effectively.

By practicing these strategies, you play a pivotal role in shaping an environment that not only nurtures but also empowers young individuals. You'll encourage them to approach their feelings with curiosity rather than fear, knowing they have a supportive listener in their corner. This creates a robust foundation for them to build upon as they navigate the complexities of their emotions.

Listening without judgment is, in essence, a gift of understanding. It reassures the child that they are respected and valued, no matter what they are experiencing. This validation is often the first crucial step toward healing, growth, and, ultimately, overcoming anxiety.

Chapter 5:
Role of Parents and Caregivers

In the journey of helping young people manage anxiety, parents and caregivers are pivotal figures. They're the anchors that provide stability and calm when the storm of anxiety rages. By fostering a safe and nurturing environment, caregivers help children navigate their feelings without fear or judgment. It's all about walking the fine line between offering support and avoiding over-protection, which could inadvertently amplify anxiety. The role extends beyond just identifying triggers; it's about equipping children with the confidence to face challenges head-on. Bringing awareness and mindfulness to everyday interactions sets a model for resilience, shaping how young minds perceive and respond to stress. This crucial support system empowers children and adolescents to develop emotional tools that will last a lifetime, reinforcing their ability to confront anxiety with courage and assurance.

Creating a Safe Space

Navigating the tempestuous waters of anxiety can be challenging for both young ones and those who care for them. As a parent or caregiver, one of the most significant roles you can play is to create a safe, secure environment where children feel comfortable exploring their emotions. The creation of a safe space isn't just about physical surroundings; it's about building an atmosphere of trust and understanding, where kids know they can express their worries without fear of judgment.

Consider the dynamics of trust first. Children need to believe that they can approach you with their concerns, no matter how small or irrational they might seem. Cultivating this trust requires consistent actions and a genuine openness to listen. Kids must see that their world isn't just predictable, but also accepting. Anchoring emotional security begins with demonstrating unconditional support, showing that their anxieties will be met with compassion.

Every interaction counts. Simple gestures, like attentive listening or a warm hug, can reinforce the idea that home is a sanctuary from the outside world's pressures. When children perceive their surroundings as safe, they're more likely to open up, giving you precious insight into their internal struggles. By being present, you're signaling that their feelings matter.

It's essential, too, to discuss feelings in an age-appropriate manner. This means using language they understand and avoiding minimizing language that diminishes their worries. Engage in conversations that normalize the discussion of emotions and ensure that your child knows it's okay to be anxious sometimes. Offering language to express what they're going through can be empowering and affirming.

Moreover, creating a safe space includes setting boundaries. Structure and routine can provide a sense of stability that eases anxiety. While it may seem counterintuitive, boundaries are a form of care that demonstrate you're in control, which can make a chaotic world feel more manageable for children.

The physical environment matters as much as the emotional one. Children should have access to spaces that encourage relaxation and reflection. This might be a cozy corner equipped with soft pillows, blankets, and perhaps books that encourage emotional literacy. A peaceful environment can serve as a physical sanctuary for kids to retreat when feelings become overwhelming.

Keep communication lines open, fostering an environment where questions are welcome, and answers are given thoughtfully. Encouraging open dialogue starts with asking the right questions, showing genuine interest in their daily experiences, and demonstrating empathy in your responses. These interactions should feel natural and not interrogative.

There's real strength in validation. Validating your child's emotions doesn't mean you always agree with their perspective, but it does mean acknowledging their right to feel a certain way. Validation helps in distinguishing between the emotion and the response, allowing kids to learn how to tackle their anxiety from a place of emotional strength.

With safety comes empowerment. Teach children that experiencing anxiety doesn't define them. When they feel secure, they can learn to decouple their identity from their anxiety, fostering resilience. It's about helping them understand that they aren't their worries; instead, they possess the ability to navigate through them.

In a safe space, mistakes become teaching moments rather than failures. Encourage them to face small fears and celebrate each courageous step forward. By doing this, you instill a sense of accomplishment and reinforce that failure is simply a part of the learning process.

Your role as a safe haven can have a lasting impact. By crafting and nurturing an environment that feels safe and supportive, you're contributing immeasurably to your child's emotional development. Such a space allows them not only to face their fears but to flourish despite them.

Ultimately, the goal is to equip them with the tools to create their own spaces of safety and resilience as they grow and encounter the world on their terms. Just as springboards help divers reach new heights, a supportive environment can launch your child into their future with confidence and courage.

In essence, creating a safe space is about connection. It's about being a beacon of hope and a pillar of support. It is your patient understanding and unwavering presence that will light their path, guiding them toward a future where anxiety doesn't hold the reins but becomes a manageable part of their rich tapestry of experience.

Supporting Without Enabling

In our roles as parents and caregivers, the line between supporting a child and enabling anxious behaviors can often feel blurred. Children and adolescents struggling with anxiety look to us for guidance, and it's our responsibility to navigate this delicate balance. We aim to support their growth and resilience while ensuring they don't become reliant on avoidance tactics that reinforce anxiety. By stepping back at the right moments, we empower them to develop their own coping skills, crucial for overcoming the challenges anxiety presents.

Enabling, in this context, can mean unintentionally reinforcing an anxious child's fears by allowing them to consistently avoid situations that provoke anxiety. While it's instinctive to protect our children from distress, chronic avoidance can hinder their ability to confront and manage their anxiety. For instance, a child afraid of social situations might be allowed to skip school events. While this might seem helpful in the short term, it doesn't teach them how to handle similar situations in the future and can increase anxiety over time.

Imagine a young person, fearful of attending a friend's birthday party. As a caregiver, encouraging them to attend, even briefly, can serve as a powerful lesson in perseverance. Offer practical strategies for how to cope during the party, such as taking deep breaths or linking up with a familiar friend upon arrival. This kind of support provides a safety net, but also nudges them toward facing their fears. It's about building bridges between comfort and challenge, helping them step across when they're ready.

Consistently helping them to confront their fears rather than avoiding them fosters resilience. It demonstrates belief in their capabilities and instills confidence. Help them understand that anxiety might show up, and that's normal, but it doesn't have to rule their lives. Sharing stories of how others have managed similar fears can be particularly motivational, illustrating that anxiety can be overcome through determination and effort.

A supportive environment is crucial. It begins with active listening. Create a space where children feel safe expressing their anxieties without fear of judgment. Validate their feelings, letting them know they're not alone in their experiences. This validation can be incredibly reassuring and can reduce feelings of isolation that often accompany anxiety.

Providing reassurance doesn't mean removing every obstacle; instead, it's about equipping young people with the right tools to climb over them. This involves helping them identify and challenge unhelpful thoughts, developing problem-solving skills, and encouraging gradual exposure to feared situations. All these techniques help build an emotional toolkit that the child can rely on throughout their lifetime.

In some cases, professional guidance might be necessary. Consulting a therapist, especially one trained in cognitive-behavioral techniques, might offer the additional support required. Therapy can guide both parents and children through the process of setting boundaries between support and enabling. Therapists can suggest structured approaches that balance empathy with empowerment, promoting self-sufficiency in children.

Bear in mind that patience and consistency are key. It might not always be easy to watch your child struggle, but through small, courageous steps forward, they're actually learning the most profound lessons. Witnessing them tackle their anxieties with increasing confidence is rewarding. It's an affirmation that, with your support guiding them away from enabling behaviors, they're becoming equipped to handle life's uncertainties independently.

Parents and caregivers should also remember to take care of themselves. Anxiety management is a journey for both children and adults. Practicing self-care enables you to be the best support system possible. When you engage in activities that reduce your stress, you promote a healthy atmosphere at home, setting a positive example for your child to follow. It's a reminder that everyone, no matter their age, can benefit from taking time to nurture their well-being.

Ultimately, supporting without enabling involves a delicate balance of empathy, guidance, and encouragement. It's about knowing when to step in, when to stand back, and how to empower your child to engage with and move through their anxiety. By doing so, you're teaching them resilience, self-confidence, and independence — gifts that will last a lifetime and equip them to handle future challenges with grace and strength.

Chapter 6:
Managing Anxiety in Daily Life

In the whirlwind of daily life, managing anxiety becomes a skill that young people and their caregivers can develop together, fostering resilience and confidence. A structured routine offers a comforting predictability, helping reduce anxiety levels by creating a safe framework within which children can thrive. Balancing school obligations with social activities teaches invaluable time management skills, turning potentially overwhelming situations into manageable experiences. As they navigate friendships, academics, and extracurricular interests, youngsters develop resilience through daily practice, gradually understanding how to prioritize tasks and set boundaries. Mastering these everyday challenges not only alleviates anxiety but also empowers children with a sense of agency, reminding them that they're capable of taking charge of their lives. By tackling anxiety one day at a time, children learn to view their feelings as manageable parts of their journey, not obstacles in their path.

Routine and Structure

In the often chaotic world of growing up, establishing a predictable routine can be a powerful antidote to anxiety. Children and adolescents, like adults, benefit greatly from knowing what to expect. It gives them a sense of control and security, something that can often feel out of reach when anxiety looms large. When their days have a reliable rhythm, it can act like a comforting lullaby that soothes an anxious mind.

Creating a routine doesn't mean turning life into a rigid schedule that allows no flexibility. It's more about setting a consistent framework where the young mind can rest. For example, having regular meal times, a consistent homework schedule, and designated times for relaxation or family activities can anchor the day. These are not just mundane tasks; they are the building blocks for a sense of stability and predictability, which are crucial for managing anxiety.

For parents and caregivers, helping children establish routines involves balancing flexibility with consistency. Kids need to learn that while routines are important, life can be unpredictable, and adaptability is a skill worth cultivating. In fact, how we respond to disruptions can teach valuable lessons about resilience and problem-solving. Teaching youngsters that it's okay for things to occasionally go off-track helps them develop a healthier relationship with uncertainty.

Consider bedtime, for instance. A bedtime routine is more than just a series of actions leading to sleep. It's a signal to the brain that the time for rest is approaching. Incorporating calming activities such as reading or a brief mindfulness exercise can ease the mind into a restful state, reducing nighttime anxiety. Over time, this consistent practice can improve sleep quality, which is often hindered by anxiety.

Establishing structure doesn't solely pertain to the home. School life can also benefit greatly from routines. Encouraging children to use planners or digital tools to keep track of assignments fosters a habit of planning and organization. This habit not only helps to ease the burden of academic responsibilities but also serves as a lifelong skill that reduces future anxiety associated with overwhelming tasks.

Moreover, incorporating regular family time can strengthen relationships and encourage open communication. A weekly family night or daily meal together can provide a safe space for children to express their feelings, knowing they have dedicated time with supportive figures. It emphasizes the family's role as a unified team against anxiety.

It's vital to acknowledge, though, that building a routine should be a collaborative process. Involving children and adolescents in planning their daily and weekly routines fosters a sense of ownership and empowerment. This not only aids in adherence but also encourages decision-making skills and personal responsibility.

Yet, routines are not a solitary solution. They work best when paired with a broader understanding of other anxiety management tools. Encouraging young people to integrate coping strategies like mindfulness or physical activity into their daily routines can further enhance their ability to manage anxiety. These strategies, explored more deeply in other sections, complement the structured environment by providing immediate practical tools for managing stress and anxiety in real-life situations.

In a world that never stops moving, embracing the power of routine and structure can feel like holding onto an anchor in stormy seas. It provides stability not only to those struggling with anxiety but also to their caregivers, who are equally riding the waves. Together, with routines in place, families can work towards a harmonious balance that champions the emotional and mental well-being of young minds.

Balancing School and Social Life

Navigating the delicate balance between school and social life is crucial for young people, especially when managing anxiety. School presents a multitude of challenges—academic pressure, social dynamics, and extracurricular commitments—that can be overwhelming. At the same time, maintaining social relationships is integral for emotional well-being, providing support, joy, and a sense of belonging. For caregivers and adolescents working to manage anxiety, finding harmony in these areas can significantly affect how anxiety is experienced and managed.

It's important to recognize that school can be both a source of stress and a fertile ground for growth. Academic work requires focus and persistence, often presenting a pressure that heightens anxiety for many children and teens. The expectations to perform well, coupled with deadlines and the sheer volume of tasks, can feel daunting. Yet, it's in these structured environments that young people can learn vital skills like time management and critical thinking. By setting realistic goals and breaking tasks into manageable parts, students can feel more in control and less overwhelmed.

However, it's not just the academics that can be anxiety-inducing. Social aspects of school life, such as interacting with peers, participating in group activities, or simply fitting in, can evoke feelings of anxiety. Navigating these situations requires social skills that aren't always innate. For some, the school cafeteria or a crowded hallway can feel like walking through a minefield. Encouraging children to engage in activities they enjoy can help them build confidence in social settings. Joining a club or a team that aligns with their interests fosters friendships within safe parameters and reduces the fear of rejection or judgment.

Outside school, social life provides an essential outlet for relaxation and joy, crucial for counterbalancing academic stress. Friends can offer perspective and emotional support, reinforcing that one is not alone in their struggles. They also provide opportunities for laughter and fun— critical components of a well-rounded, anxiety-managed life. Being social isn't just about having fun; it's an essential means to develop empathy and communication skills, buffers against the isolation that often accompanies anxiety.

That said, striking the right balance is pivotal. Overcommitting to social activities can lead to exhaustion and prevent focus on academics, while focusing solely on school can lead to burnout and social isolation. Helping young people understand their limits and encouraging them to prioritize their commitments can aid in achieving this balance. It's about finding what personally works for them, which can be different for each individual.

Routine and structure play essential roles in balancing these aspects of life. Establishing a schedule that allows time for study, hobbies, and relaxation can provide predictability and control, reducing overall anxiety. For those in high school, it might involve homework after school, then participating in a favorite hobby or sport, leaving time for friends and family over the weekend. For younger children, regular routines involving study, play, and downtime can help them feel secure and manage expectations better.

Open communication between caregivers and young people is fundamental. When children and teens feel safe discussing their concerns, they are more likely to express when they feel overwhelmed or need help re-evaluating their commitments. Caregivers can encourage these conversations by actively listening and offering non-judgmental feedback, enabling children to explore solutions that best fit their needs. Asking open-ended questions like "How do you feel about the time you spend on different activities?" can prompt self-reflection and lead to better personal management of school and social life balance.

Technology, while often disparaged in discussions about youth anxiety, can also be a powerful tool for maintaining balance. Calendar apps can help organize commitments, while group chats allow friendships to flourish even when face-to-face interaction isn't possible. Nevertheless, setting boundaries for technology use is essential to ensure it serves as a tool, not a source of additional stress.

Navigating school and social life balance also calls for flexibility and adaptability. Life is dynamic, with shifting priorities and unexpected challenges, and being able to adjust when necessary is central to managing anxiety. This resilience is something that can be taught and nurtured. By encouraging young people to view setbacks not as failures but as opportunities for growth, we cultivate a mindset that can approach changes with confidence and reduced anxiety.

Throughout this journey, it is crucial for caregivers to role model effective balancing strategies themselves. Demonstrating positive time management and a balanced outlook on work and relaxation can significantly impact children. When caregivers show how they balance their responsibilities and leisure, it reinforces healthy habits and resilience-building strategies in young minds.

Ultimately, the goal is not to eliminate anxiety but to equip young people with the tools to manage it effectively. By balancing school and social life, they build the confidence and resilience needed to face whatever challenges come their way. Supporting young people as they find their balance allows them to thrive not only academically and socially but in every facet of their lives.

Chapter 7:
Conquering Specific Fears

In the journey of guiding young minds through the labyrinth of anxiety, tackling specific fears can feel like scaling individual peaks of a daunting mountain range. Each fear, be it of heights, darkness, or social situations, brings its unique challenges and opportunities for growth. To effectively conquer these fears, it's essential to blend understanding and strategy. Delve into the nature of phobias with empathy, recognizing them as learned responses that can be unlearned through patience and dedication. Gradual exposure techniques offer a transformative approach, encouraging young people to face fears incrementally, building confidence with each small step. By creating a supportive environment filled with compassion and unwavering encouragement, parents and caregivers can empower children to transform fear into fuel for personal development. Celebrate every milestone, no matter how small, as it strengthens resilience and fosters a mindset that embraces challenges as opportunities. Through this supportive process, young individuals not only conquer specific fears but also cultivate a broad resilience that equips them for life's myriad tests.

Understanding Phobias

Phobias are intense, often irrational fears that can seem puzzling both to those who experience them and to the people around them. These specific fears sometimes appear in surprising forms, manifesting in ways that feel uncontrollable. To parents, caregivers, and young people themselves, phobias might seem like an insurmountable barrier. But understanding the nature of these fears is the first step toward conquering them.

Life for a young person can be overwhelming enough as it is, without the added weight of a phobia. A child might suddenly develop an overpowering fear of dogs, elevators, or heights, which may seem trivial to others but feel entirely consuming to them. Such fears can limit their experiences and stifle their chances to explore the world. Recognizing these phobias for what they are—a type of anxiety disorder—can guide us toward more effective responses and solutions.

Phobias differentiate themselves from everyday fears by their intensity and the degree to which they disrupt daily activities. Imagine a young person who cannot walk past a neighbor's dog without feeling their heart race. They may avoid the dog's route altogether, even if it means going completely out of their way. This avoidance is a hallmark of phobias—a persistent need to distance themselves from whatever they're irrationally afraid of.

What is it that makes a particular object or situation so terrifying? The origins of phobias are as varied as the individuals who experience them. Sometimes, a traumatic event involving the feared object or situation ignites a phobia. For example, a bad fall from a tree might spark a fear of heights. Genetics and environmental factors also play crucial roles, interacting in complex ways to shape these specific fears. Understanding the roots of a phobia can help demystify it, making it seem less formidable.

Knowing the nature of phobias allows us to develop strategies to help young people face them. Gradual exposure techniques, which will be discussed further in the upcoming section, can play an instrumental role in this process. By slowly and safely exposing individuals to the source of their fear, these techniques help reduce anxiety levels over time.

The emotional toolkit built in previous chapters becomes paramount when dealing with phobias. Encouraging children to articulate their fears can lighten the burden of carrying them in silence. When a child can voice what specifically they fear, the fear itself becomes more manageable. Awareness is a powerful tool; it transforms a nebulous source of anxiety into something tangible and, thus, more addressable.

In our quest to understand phobias, we mustn't forget the power of empathy. As parents and caregivers, providing a strong support network for young people grappling with phobias is key. Creating a safe space where they feel heard and understood can have an immeasurable impact. At times, the most healing factor is simply knowing they're not alone on this journey.

For young people, phobias can feel isolating. The perception of being different or 'other' can exacerbate fears even more. It's crucial to remind them that phobias are a common experience and having them doesn't reflect a personal failing. Many individuals—children and adults alike—navigate life successfully while managing their specific fears, and plenty more find ways to overcome them entirely.

While phobias can indeed be debilitating, enlightenment on this topic provides a ray of hope. Knowledge can transform how a young person perceives their fear, diminishing its power over them. Rather than allowing it to dictate their life's boundaries, understanding offers the opportunity to redraw those lines, expanding their horizons.

Young people shouldn't see phobias as permanent fixtures in their lives. Instead, with the right tools, they can learn to confront their fears head-on and gradually dismantle the hold these phobias have over them. Developing a resilient mindset towards phobias can empower them to tackle not just these specific fears, but all manners of anxiety that may arise throughout their lives.

As we move forward in this journey, we will explore various techniques and methods—like gradual exposure—that can be employed to confront phobias. With a growing understanding of these fears and a toolkit crafted for emotional resilience, young people and those who care for them will be well-equipped to create brave new paths regardless of the shadows that once loomed large. Understanding is indeed the first step; action follows next in reshaping fear into freedom.

Gradual Exposure Techniques

Conquering specific fears can feel like a mountain to climb. But what if we took it one step at a time, adjusting our gait to the incline in a way that's gentle and manageable? That's where gradual exposure techniques come in. With a steady approach, children and adolescents can slowly face the fears that seem to overshadow their world. This isn't about diving into the deep end; it's about dipping a toe into the water until confidence grows and fear diminishes.

Imagine a child who's terrified of dogs, despite these furry friends often being delightful companions. Plunging them into a park filled with canines could amplify the anxiety. Instead, start with something more approachable—looking at photos of dogs, for instance. Over time, they might watch videos, then see a dog from a distance, and eventually get close enough to pet one on a leash. Each step is carefully calibrated, allowing the child to adjust emotionally and cognitively, revealing that fears, much like shadows, aren't as intimidating once faced directly.

Gradual exposure techniques are rooted in cognitive-behavioral therapy and rely on the concept of desensitization. By repeatedly facing a feared object or situation in a controlled and progressive way, the individual learns that the fear can be mastered and the anticipated distress doesn't always match reality. This gradual buildup is like climbing a ladder—each rung leads to greater understanding and control.

With gradual exposure, it's crucial to tailor the approach to each child's comfort level and specific fears. What works for one child might not suit another, even if the fears appear similar on the surface. Start with collaboration to discuss and map out the steps. Involving the child in this process gives them a sense of control, transforming fear from an insurmountable force to something they can manage. This fosters a partnership where the child is an active participant in their journey rather than a passive recipient.

Creating a fear hierarchy is often the first step. List the fears from the least frightening to the most anxiety-inducing. A visual aid—a ladder or pyramid—can help make this process tangible. Assure the child that the pace of climbing is entirely in their hands. Saying "no" to a harder step isn't failing; it's a strategic choice that respects their emotional readiness. This hierarchy provides a roadmap, and while detours happen, the end goal remains steady.

As exposure begins, it's critical to monitor and acknowledge feelings. Encourage the child to note their emotional and physical reactions. Learning to identify these signs is empowering—it demystifies what has previously been overwhelming. It's also important to remind them that discomfort is part of the process and does not signify danger or failure. Celebrating small victories at each step reinforces progress and builds self-esteem.

However, gradual exposure isn't moving forward blindly. The pace must be aligned with the child's emotional rhythm. An emotional toolkit filled with coping strategies—such as mindful breathing or positive self-talk—is valuable. Whenever anxiety spikes during exposure, these tools can help reground the child, serving both as a safety net and a launchpad.

Supportive caregivers bring immense value to this process. Your presence offers reassurance and accountability. You're not just a guide but a cheerleader, celebrating wins and providing comfort when setbacks occur. Your patience is crucial—there's no rush. The aim is lasting change and growth, not a quick fix. Encourage the child's voice and let them express how each step feels. This open communication ensures adjustments can be made to the pace and approach.

Remember, setbacks on this journey are opportunities for learning and resilience building. They provide a chance to review strategies, explore emotions, and reprioritize goals. There's immense power in reframing setbacks as integral components of progress rather than failures. Emphasize to the child that being courageous doesn't mean the absence of fear, but rather the decision to move forward in spite of it.

Gradual exposure techniques are a journey towards mastery. They embrace the human capacity for growth and transformation. As children learn to tackle their fears incrementally, they gain skills that extend beyond the specific phobia. These skills embolden them to face unknown challenges throughout life. By fostering these experiences, you're helping build a resilient mindset. The once towering mountain becomes a series of manageable hills, ready for exploration and conquest.

With time, patience, and encouragement, the goals outlined in the fear hierarchy become milestones of achievement. Each conquered fear adds to a growing sense of independence and self-assurance. It's a journey that fosters not just the management of anxiety but enhances overall confidence and resilience. These gradual steps transform lives, each small victory leaving an enduring mark of courage.

Chapter 8:
The Power of Mindfulness

In the journey of navigating anxiety, mindfulness emerges as a profound ally, particularly for young minds still sculpting their understanding of the world and themselves. By introducing mindfulness practices, we offer children and adolescents an anchor amidst life's uncertainties, helping them to find calm in the often-stormy seas of anxiety. Engaging in mindful breathing allows them to reconnect with the present moment, reducing the grip of anxious thoughts and fostering a sense of inner peace and clarity. As they practice, children begin to notice the subtle shifts within their bodies and minds, cultivating self-awareness and emotional regulation. This practice is not just about breath or stillness; it's a powerful way to build resilience and confidence, equipping young individuals with a toolkit to manage anxiety throughout life's many challenges. By encouraging mindfulness, caregivers empower young people to embrace their experiences with courage and curiosity, transforming anxiety into a pathway for growth and self-discovery.

Introducing Mindfulness Practices

Mindfulness, a practice deeply rooted in ancient traditions, offers a refreshing perspective in today's fast-paced world. At its core, it's about bringing one's attention to the present moment without judgment. It's an exercise in awareness, a shift from the usual autopilot way of living that modern society often demands. Introducing mindfulness to young individuals, especially those grappling with anxiety, can be a game-changer. It has the potential to ground them amidst life's turbulent storms, offering them a sanctuary of calm and clarity.

For parents and caregivers, incorporating mindfulness into a child's life can start with something as simple as mindful breathing. This foundational practice doesn't require a specific place or time; it can be done anywhere, anytime. Encourage your child to take a moment to sit quietly, focus on their breathing, and notice how it feels to breathe in and out. This practice, though simple, can have profound effects on their mental state. It serves as a tool to center themselves when anxiety starts to creep in.

A key element of mindfulness is focusing on the sensory experiences around you. For children, this can be as straightforward as paying attention to the sound of leaves rustling, the feeling of a breeze against their skin, or the taste of their lunch. Engage them in activities like a mindful walk, where they notice every detail of their surroundings—the sights, the sounds, the smells. These exercises don't just distract them from their worries; they anchor them in the now, shifting their concentration away from distressing thoughts to more tangible, less anxiety-inducing experiences.

Incorporating play is another effective way. Activities like coloring, crafting, or building with blocks can be incredibly soothing. When children focus on these tasks, they are effortlessly practicing mindfulness. Engage them by asking questions about the colors they choose or the structures they build. This approach opens a space for creative expression and mindfulness simultaneously. As they become absorbed in these activities, they also learn to appreciate moments of stillness and focus, skills that are vital for managing anxiety.

Meditation, though often considered more advanced, can be simplified for young minds. Guided meditations specifically crafted for children use visualization techniques—imagining a peaceful place or a favorite activity—to foster relaxation and concentration. These visual journeys can be a sanctuary where they learn to harness their imagination positively and find inner peace. Start with short sessions, gradually increasing the duration as they become more comfortable.

Another practice that can be tailored is body scanning. A gentle technique that brings awareness to different parts of the body, it helps children recognize areas of tension and encourages relaxation. As they mentally scan from head to toe, they learn to identify where they hold stress and find ways to release it. This practice not only promotes relaxation but also enhances their ability to tune into their bodies and emotions, offering insights into how anxiety physically manifests.

Gratitude exercises can also embed mindfulness into everyday life. Encourage your child to think about or write down three things they are thankful for each day. This simple practice shifts focus from anxiety to positivity, fostering a mindset centered around appreciation and abundance. Over time, this shift can help create lasting changes in how children perceive and respond to stressors.

Mindful listening is a practice that deeply benefits children. In a world filled with noise and distraction, teaching them to truly listen— whether it be to their favorite song, the sound of nature, or even a parent's voice—can enhance their focus and calmness. It encourages them to engage fully with what they hear, pulling them away from anxious thoughts and into the richness of their auditory experiences.

Connecting mindfulness with daily routines is another useful strategy. Whether it's mindful eating, where they savor each bite, noticing the texture and flavors, or mindful dressing, paying attention to the feel of clothes on their skin, these practices help embed mindfulness into their daily lives without adding additional demands. It teaches them to approach everyday tasks with intention, reducing mental clutter and cultivating presence.

Storytelling and reading can also incorporate mindfulness. Choose stories where characters display resilience and mindfulness, encouraging children to reflect on these themes. Ask them questions like how a character handled a stressful situation and what they might have done differently. Such discussions not only enhance comprehension and empathy but also model mindfulness in problem-solving and emotional regulation.

Beyond individual practices, incorporating mindfulness into family activities can strengthen bonds while promoting well-being. Set aside time for mindful family walks, yoga sessions, or meditation circles. These shared experiences build a supportive environment where mindfulness is not just a practice but a way of living. Moreover, it allows children to see adults modeling healthy stress management, which reinforces their learning.

In integrating these mindfulness practices, remember to approach it with patience and kindness. It's not about forcing compliance but fostering curiosity and openness. Support your child's journey with encouragement and lead by example. Mindfulness is a skill, and like any other, it takes time to develop. Over time, these practices can transform how children interact with their anxieties, equipping them with a toolkit that promotes resilience, confidence, and a greater sense of peace. By embedding these habits early, you offer not just immediate relief but lay the foundation for lifelong emotional well-being.

Benefits of Mindful Breathing

Mindful breathing may sound simple, but its power is profound. In a world where young minds are often overwhelmed by stress and anxiety, introducing such a practice can be transformative. It doesn't just teach children how to breathe properly; it gifts them a tool for life, offering both immediate relief from anxiety and long-term resilience.

One of the immediate benefits of mindful breathing is its ability to calm the nervous system. When children focus on their breath, they activate the body's relaxation response. This is particularly useful in moments of acute stress or anxiety, providing a way to quickly regain composure. By engaging in deep, slow breathing, they decrease their heart rate and lower stress hormone levels, which can create an immediate sense of peace.

As young people learn to focus on their breathing, they also develop a heightened sense of self-awareness. This is crucial because recognizing and understanding their emotional and physical reactions to stress is the first step in managing these responses. Mindful breathing encourages this awareness without judgment, cultivating a habit of observing oneself with kindness and curiosity. This nurtures an open dialogue within themselves, which can extend to conversations with others.

Beyond the immediate physiological benefits, mindful breathing contributes to emotional regulation. Young people who practice controlled breathing often find it easier to regulate their emotions. This is because mindful breathing provides a pause between impulse and reaction. In moments of conflict or emotional intensity, taking a step back to breathe mindfully can prevent rash decisions or reactions, leading to more thoughtful, considered actions.

The practice of mindful breathing also sharpens focus and concentration. In our fast-paced, distraction-filled world, the ability to concentrate is an increasingly valuable skill. By dedicating time to focus solely on the breath, children and adolescents train their attention like a muscle, improving their capacity to concentrate in school and other activities. This improved focus helps them manage tasks more effectively and boosts academic performance, thereby reducing school-related anxiety.

In addition to the mental benefits, mindful breathing enhances physical health. Regular practice can lead to improved lung function, better circulation, and a decrease in tension-related physical symptoms such as headaches or stomachaches. These health improvements contribute to overall well-being and resilience, making children better equipped to handle life's challenges.

Moreover, mindful breathing can transform the parent-child relationship. When both parties practice together, it creates a shared space of calm and understanding. Parents modeling the practice can be particularly influential, as children often learn coping strategies by observing adults. This shared activity can strengthen bonds and build a supportive environment where anxiety feels more manageable.

Introducing mindful breathing to a child's routine is straightforward and doesn't require any special equipment. The simplicity of the practice is part of its beauty. It can be integrated into daily activities such as before homework, during commutes, or right before bed. As it becomes a familiar part of the day, the comfort and security it provides grow stronger.

The practice is also adaptable to various situations, from school settings to social environments. Imagine a child feeling anxious before a big test or nervous due to peer pressure. A few moments of mindful breathing can center them, offering clarity and confidence. It can also be a quiet companion during times of uncertainty or change, fostering adaptability and courage.

Lastly, mindful breathing is a gateway to other mindfulness practices. As children become comfortable with their breath, they may explore other techniques such as guided imagery or mindful movement, expanding their toolkit for managing anxiety and stress. Through these practices, the goal is not just to manage anxiety but to cultivate a long-term sense of inner peace and resilience.

The benefits of mindful breathing extend far beyond the practice itself, rippling out into every facet of a young person's life. It provides foundational skills for emotional and mental well-being and opens doors to greater self-awareness, improved relationships, and enhanced life satisfaction. In teaching a child to breathe mindfully, we empower them with a timeless strategy for navigating the world with grace and confidence.

Chapter 9:
Cognitive Behavioral Techniques

In the journey of understanding and managing anxiety, it's crucial to harness the power of cognitive behavioral techniques. These strategies empower young people to identify and challenge the negative thoughts that often fuel their anxieties. By consciously shifting their mindset, they can gradually replace these patterns with positive thoughts that build self-assurance and resilience. The process might seem daunting at first, but with practice, it transforms into an invaluable life skill. It's about recognizing that thoughts aren't facts—they're just perceptions we can reshape. By encouraging children and adolescents to explore this truth, caregivers and parents can nurture an environment where hope thrives over fear, and constructive thinking becomes a natural reflex. This approach not only adapts to the unique journey of each child but also lays a foundation for mental sturdiness that will support them throughout their lives. Embracing these techniques can be a cornerstone in fostering an optimistic outlook, turning the tables on anxiety and sparking a renewed sense of control and confidence in young minds.

Challenging Negative Thoughts

Anxiety often stems from a tangled web of negative thoughts. These thoughts can weave patterns in the minds of young people that obscure reality, making it difficult for them to see the brighter, more hopeful perspectives. It's crucial for parents, caregivers, and young people themselves to recognize and challenge these negative thought patterns. By doing so, they can unravel anxiety's grip, allowing room for healthier, more balanced thinking.

Negative thoughts can appear insidious and relentless, gnawing at the edges of a child's self-esteem or distorting their perception of events. Imagine a child who constantly thinks, "I'm not good enough" or "Something bad will happen." These aren't just fleeting concerns; they can become deeply embedded beliefs that hinder the child's ability to navigate everyday life. Challenging these thoughts involves understanding their origin and questioning their validity.

One effective technique to confront negative thinking is *cognitive restructuring*. This method encourages children to identify irrational or unhelpful thoughts and transform them into more realistic and positive ones. To begin this process, it's helpful to teach young individuals to recognize the automatic nature of these negative thoughts. They often spring up reflexively in stressful situations, bypassing logical analysis. By writing these thoughts down, children can pause and examine them critically.

Consider the story of a young girl named Emma who struggled with the fear of failing in school. Her anxiety whispered to her, "If I don't get an A, I'm a failure." Through cognitive restructuring, she learned to challenge this belief. Her caregivers guided her to question: "What evidence do I have that supports this thought?" and "What evidence counters it?" Emma discovered that her worth wasn't tied to a single grade, allowing her to view challenges in her schoolwork as opportunities for learning rather than as threats to her self-worth.

Another useful approach is to evaluate the **catastrophic thinking** that can so often accompany anxiety. Children may leap to the worst-case scenario in their minds, believing that any small mistake could lead to disaster. Encouraging them to play the "What if?" game in reverse can be illuminating. Ask them to consider, "What if everything worked out fine?" or "What if it's not as bad as it seems?" This shift in perspective can offer a way out of the catastrophizing spiral.

A vital part of challenging negative thoughts is fostering an inquisitive mindset. Curiosity invites children to explore their emotional responses with a sense of wonder and non-judgment. When they approach their anxieties with curiosity, it becomes easier to separate the anxious thought from the reality of the situation. For example, instead of accepting "I'm going to embarrass myself," they could ask, "What if people appreciate my effort?" or "How would I respond if I saw someone else in my situation?"

The support of caregivers in this journey is crucial. Children look to their parents and guardians not just for reassurance, but for models of how to handle anxiety. By demonstrating how to calmly and rationally challenge their own negative thoughts, adults can provide children with a living blueprint on managing those disquieting voices that threaten their peace.

Equally important is encouraging positive thought patterns to replace the negative ones being challenged. This doesn't mean promoting blind optimism—rather, it's about nurturing a balanced perspective. Encourage children to focus on their strengths, achievements, and the positive aspects of their lives, leading to a more rounded self-view that resists the encroachment of negativity.

Visualization can be another powerful tool. By helping children imagine they are turning down the volume of their critical inner voice while turning up the voice that speaks in support of their efforts and potential, they can gain control over their thoughts. Role-playing scenarios where their positive self-voice takes center stage can build confidence and resilience.

Storytelling, whether through reading or writing, also aids in confronting and reshaping negative thoughts. By relating their experiences to characters or writing their own narratives where they overcome challenges, children can see their journeys as ongoing stories of growth and resilience. This not only helps in reframing negative thoughts but also empowers them with the sense that they are active participants in their life story.

In conclusion, challenging negative thoughts is more than a technique; it's a transformative journey. It's about equipping young minds with tools to dismantle the barriers negative thinking erects and replace them with bridges to knowledge, self-acceptance, and hope. In nurturing this skill, we're preparing children to face anxiety head-on, not with fear but with courage, understanding, and a belief in their own capacity to shape their thoughts and, consequently, their lives.

Building Positive Thought Patterns

For many young people grappling with anxiety, the mind often becomes a battlefield of negative thoughts. These involuntary ideas can fuel fears, make everyday challenges seem insurmountable, and lead to feelings of helplessness. Yet, the power to reshape one's thoughts lies within reach, a central concept in cognitive behavioral techniques. By intentionally redirecting thought patterns from gloomy to bright, we can help children and adolescents develop mental resilience and a more optimistic outlook on life. This transformative process isn't instantaneous, but with consistent practice, its effectiveness becomes evident.

To start building positive thought patterns, it's vital to first recognize the pervasive nature of negative thinking. Many children aren't even aware that their thoughts skew negative, which can create a cycle of self-fulfilling prophecies. Encouraging awareness is the initial step in breaking this cycle. Ask them to observe their thoughts as if watching clouds drift by, acknowledging each one without judgment.

This practice fosters an understanding of their mental landscape and empowers them to notice patterns that may not serve them well.

After this stage of recognition, the next step involves challenging negative thoughts actively. It's essential to teach young people how to question the validity of their thoughts. Are these thoughts based on facts or assumptions? Could there be another perspective? By adopting a curious yet skeptical mindset, children learn not to take every thought at face value. They begin to understand that not all thoughts are truths, and they hold the power to reframe them in a more positive light.

Reframing is a skill that flourishes with practice. One effective technique involves teaching children to replace negative thoughts with positive or neutral alternatives. If a child thinks, "I'll definitely fail the test," guide them to consider, "I've prepared as best as I can, and that's what matters." This shift isn't about dismissing valid concerns but rather about nurturing a balanced perspective that includes positive possibilities.

Create a 'positivity journal' where children can record instances of successful rethinking. By physically writing down their challenges and how they turned them around, children can visually see their progress. Over time, these written experiences act as evidence of their capability to overcome adversity, reinforcing the belief that their thoughts and behaviors are under their control.

Moreover, affirmations play an integral role in solidifying positive thought patterns. Encourage children to develop a set of affirmations that resonate with them, like "I am capable" or "Today is a new opportunity." Reciting these phrases daily, even when they don't entirely believe them at first, can gradually instill a sense of self-worth and strength. The power of repetition in learning is well-documented; applying it to our self-dialogue is no different.

Equally important is creating an environment that supports positivity. Parents and caregivers can model constructive thinking through their daily interactions. When adults demonstrate resilience and optimism in the face of challenges, children observe and internalize these reactions as normative behavior. It's crucial for adults to share their own experiences with reframing negative thoughts, making the learning process collaborative and relatable.

Incorporating exercises that promote gratitude can also enhance a child's ability to build positive thought patterns. Encouraging children to list things they're grateful for, no matter how seemingly insignificant, can reorient the mind towards positivity. As they regularly engage in this practice, they'll find it easier to notice and appreciate the good, even during adversities.

Consistent engagement in these methods fosters a shift from entrenched negative thought patterns to more flexible, positive ones. Over time, children develop the habit of automatically challenging negative thoughts and considering more constructive alternatives. This foundation of positive thinking will serve them well throughout adolescence and beyond, equipping them with a toolkit to handle life's myriad challenges gracefully and with hope.

Ultimately, building positive thought patterns isn't about ignoring or invalidating difficult emotions. It's about empowering young people to take control of their narrative and choose thoughts that propel them forward rather than holding them back. Through patience and persistent practice, the journey towards optimistic thinking becomes one of self-discovery and empowerment. By mastering this cognitive skill, young individuals not only learn to face their anxieties but also gain the confidence to lead fulfilling, resilient lives.

Chapter 10:
Dealing with Social Anxiety

Social anxiety can cast a long shadow over the vibrant social experiences that should fill a young person's life, yet understanding and confronting it can unlock doors to meaningful connections and confidence. At its core, social anxiety often stems from a fear of judgment or rejection, causing children and adolescents to avoid social situations that ignite these fears. By gradually encouraging children to step out of their comfort zones, they begin to see social interactions not as daunting tasks but as opportunities for growth and self-expression. Parents and caregivers play a pivotal role in this process by modeling grace under pressure and helping their children embrace imperfections. Practicing and mastering just a few social interactions each day, and relishing small victories, can slowly but surely build resilience. Those facing social anxiety are not alone; with patience and the right strategies, they can flourish in any social setting, paving the way for fulfilling relationships and a brighter, more confident future.

Navigating Peer Pressure

Social anxiety can feel like an insurmountable obstacle for many young people, especially when compounded by the pressures of fitting in and meeting the expectations of peers. Peer pressure is a potent force that can influence choices, behavior, and self-perception. It's crucial to understand how this dynamic works and find ways to navigate it effectively.

For most adolescents, the desire to belong is strong. It's a time when forming connections and identifying with social groups become significant aspects of life. Peer pressure isn't inherently negative; it can sometimes promote positive behaviors, like encouraging participation in extracurricular activities or supporting academic achievements. However, when peer pressure leads to stress and anxiety, it becomes a problem that needs addressing.

Understanding the roots of peer pressure helps to manage its impact. One factor is the fear of rejection or judgment, which can drive young people to compromise their own beliefs or comfort levels just to avoid being ostracized. This fear often stems from social anxiety, making it essential for parents and caregivers to acknowledge these feelings and provide reassurance that acceptance isn't always contingent on conformity.

Sharing stories and examples of individuals who have successfully overcome peer pressure can be a powerful motivator. These stories illustrate that staying true to oneself is possible and often leads to deeper, more genuine connections. Encouraging young people to focus on their values and what truly matters to them can provide the clarity needed to resist unwanted influences.

Building resilience to peer pressure often involves cultivating a strong sense of self. Helping children and adolescents explore their interests, strengths, and values is a pivotal step. When they have a solid understanding of who they are and what they want, it's easier for them to voice their boundaries. This self-awareness acts as an anchor amidst the ever-changing social tides.

An essential part of this journey is teaching young people the skill of assertiveness. Being assertive doesn't mean being confrontational or aggressive; rather, it means expressing one's thoughts and feelings confidently and respectfully. Role-playing scenarios where they practice saying "no" or expressing a different opinion in a safe environment can boost their confidence. These skills are invaluable not only for resisting negative peer pressure but for everyday interactions.

Open communication between young people and their caregivers is another critical component in navigating peer pressure. Discussing potential scenarios and possible responses can prepare them for real-life situations. Parents and caregivers should emphasize that it's okay to seek advice or assistance when they feel overwhelmed by peer pressure. Knowing that they have a supportive network is reassuring.

Caregivers can also help by nurturing a supportive peer environment. Encourage young people to seek out friendships with those who respect their opinions and choices. A strong, positive friend group can act as a buffer against adverse influences. It's also helpful to expose them to a variety of activities and interests, promoting a sense of belonging that isn't solely reliant on peer approval.

Moreover, it's important to address any feelings of shame or embarrassment that young people might experience when they do succumb to peer pressure. These emotions can exacerbate social anxiety. Encouraging an atmosphere of forgiveness and learning from mistakes can cultivate resilience, helping them become more prepared for future challenges.

Lastly, parents and caregivers must remember the importance of modeling behavior. By demonstrating authenticity and integrity in their own lives, adults can teach young people to value these traits. When caregivers handle their own social interactions with grace and confidence, they provide a living example of how to navigate peer pressure.

Navigating peer pressure isn't just about resistance; it's about empowerment. By fostering a supportive environment and building essential skills, young people can learn to stand firm in their identities and make choices that align with their true selves. In doing so, they build not only resilience to peer pressure but also a robust framework for dealing with social anxiety overall.

Building Social Confidence

Social confidence doesn't just happen overnight, especially for young people grappling with anxiety. It's a gradual process of self-discovery, supported by knowledge and practice. Consider social confidence as a muscle: the more you exercise it, the stronger it gets. Unlike physical muscles though, this type of confidence grows with internal and external support, understanding, and the courage to step out of one's comfort zone.

For children and adolescents, stepping into social situations can be daunting. From joining a new club at school to speaking in front of classmates, the fear of being judged or misunderstood can be overwhelming. But the reality is, social interactions are an integral part of life and overcoming anxiety in these situations is crucial. By nurturing social confidence, young people can transform initial discomfort into positive, rewarding experiences.

One effective strategy in building social confidence is through role-playing scenarios. By simulating potential social interactions in a controlled environment, it allows children to practice and develop responses to different social cues. This not only familiarizes them with the social script but also empowers them to think on their feet. Encourage them to act out various scenarios, from introducing themselves to engaging in small talk; this can demystify the experience and reduce anxiety.

Moreover, fostering a growth mindset plays a significant role in social confidence. Young individuals often internalize social setbacks as reflections of personal inadequacy. However, understanding that social skills can be developed through persistence and effort—that they aren't fixed traits—can shift their perspective. Reinforce the idea that mistakes are part of learning, and every social interaction is an opportunity to grow and improve.

Building social confidence also involves setting achievable goals. Encourage youngsters to start with manageable social challenges before moving on to more complex ones. For instance, making eye contact, smiling at a peer, or offering a simple greeting can be initial steps. Celebrate these small wins, reinforcing their bravery and progress. Over time, they'll find themselves ready to engage more fully—a reminder of their capability and growth.

An often-overlooked aspect of social confidence is the importance of listening. Teaching children to be good listeners provides them with vital social skills. Emphasize active listening—maintaining eye contact, nodding in understanding, and asking follow-up questions. This not only enhances their social interactions but also boosts their confidence, knowing they can make meaningful connections.

It's crucial to cultivate an environment where self-expression is encouraged and celebrated. Whether through art, music, or storytelling, these outlets enable young individuals to communicate their thoughts and feelings creatively. This also teaches them that their voice matters and instills the confidence to say what they believe in social settings. Encouraging authentic self-expression strengthens their ability to navigate social landscapes with poise and assurance.

Of course, social confidence isn't built in isolation. Parents, caregivers, and mentors play a pivotal role by offering consistent encouragement and support. Be present and available to discuss their fears and anxieties. Highlighting their strengths and acknowledging their efforts fosters a supportive backdrop where young people can thrive socially. Remember, your belief in their abilities can be a powerful motivator.

Developing social confidence aligns closely with understanding and challenging negative thoughts about oneself. Guides or mini-workshops on positive self-talk can be immensely beneficial. Encourage the youth to identify and reframe negative thoughts by focusing on their abilities and past successes. This practice boosts their self-esteem, essential for navigating social spaces confidently.

Mindfulness techniques can also contribute significantly to building social confidence. Practices such as mindful breathing or visualization before entering social situations can help calm nerves and center focus. These techniques teach young individuals to be present in the moment, reducing anxiety about the past or future, and enabling them to engage with a steady mind.

Building social confidence is intertwined with encouraging individuality and embracing diversity. Promote the idea that being different is valuable, and their unique traits can be assets in social interactions. Encouraging diversity allows them to feel more at ease in their own skin and forms a powerfully inclusive environment where they feel a part of the collective social fabric.

Ultimately, building social confidence involves a blend of practice, persistence, and an understanding community. By nurturing these traits, young people can navigate their social worlds with increased ease and assurance, adding to their overall resilience. It's a journey of empowerment, enabling them to embrace their full potential and engage with life's social aspects with confidence and grace.

Chapter 11:
Technology and Anxiety

A s the digital age continues to advance, technology becomes both a friend and foe in the dance with anxiety among young minds. It's undeniable that social media platforms offer unprecedented opportunities for connection and self-expression, yet they often become shadowy arenas where comparison and judgment thrive. Young people, navigating these paradoxical waters, might find themselves caught in the undertow of likes, follows, and filtered realities, exacerbating feelings of inadequacy or isolation. To combat this, establishing healthy digital boundaries is crucial. It's not just about limiting screen time, but about cultivating a mindful approach to technology that prioritizes real-world connections, self-reflection, and balance. Encouraging kids and teens to unplug and engage in activities that ground them in the present—whether it's through nature, physical activities, or face-to-face interactions—can significantly diffuse anxiety tied to the online world. By fostering a healthier relationship with technology, caregivers and young people can transform it from a source of stress into a tool for empowerment and resilience.

Impact of Social Media

In today's digital age, social media is a double-edged sword for children and adolescents. It's a platform that can connect, inspire, and entertain; yet, it simultaneously harbors potential pitfalls that may contribute to a young person's anxiety. With constant notifications and the steady stream of curated content, social media can become overwhelming. Numerous studies show that excessive use of these platforms might exacerbate feelings of inadequacy, isolation, and anxiety, particularly in young, impressionable minds. Understanding these effects is crucial in helping children and adolescents manage their mental health in the digital world.

At the heart of social media lies *connection*. Teens today can stay in touch with friends, share their lives, and express themselves more freely than ever before. For many, these platforms are a modern-day lifeline, offering supportive communities where young people feel understood and valued. However, this connectivity often comes at a cost. When children scroll through carefully filtered images and idealized portrayals of life, they may begin to compare themselves unfavorably to others. This relentless comparison can foster feelings of inadequacy and anxiety as they strive to meet unrealistic standards.

The nature of social media itself—designed for continuous engagement—can lead to challenges in regulating its use. The allure of likes, comments, and shares can cause young people to constantly check their devices, creating a cycle of dependency that's hard to break. The anticipation of social feedback transforms each interaction into a potential source of stress. This cycle perpetuates anxiety when the feedback isn't what they expected or desired, turning their quest for social validation into a pressure that compounds their worry.

Social media is also a breeding ground for **cyberbullying**, which can have devastating effects on young mental health. Unlike traditional bullying, which ends once a child leaves the vicinity of their aggressor, cyberbullying can permeate every aspect of a young person's day-to-day life. Victims might feel trapped, unable to escape the judgment or harassment they encounter online, heightening feelings of anxiety and insecurity. Addressing this issue requires open communication and vigilance from parents and caregivers to ensure that children feel safe and secure in all their interactions, online or offline.

Furthermore, the fear of missing out, commonly known as FOMO, is another anxiety-inducing byproduct of social media. Seeing friends or peers engage in activities they weren't invited to or weren't able to participate in can trigger a sense of exclusion and anxiety. This perpetual notion of missing out leads young individuals to compulsively keep up with their social media feeds, fearing they'll be left out of crucial social moments or conversations. It's essential for them to recognize that each person's life is unique, and to cultivate a sense of contentment in their own experiences.

Importantly, parents and caregivers play a pivotal role in helping young people navigate the complexities of social media. By forging an open dialogue about online experiences, caregivers can help adolescents strike a balance between digital life and real-world interactions. Encouraging young people to take controlled breaks from their screens, promoting in-person connections, and guiding them towards meaningful content online can significantly mitigate the adverse impacts of social media.

Monitoring social media usage isn't about exerting control but rather about promoting **awareness and intention**. Helping young individuals develop critical thinking skills around social media can empower them to make informed decisions about the content they consume and share. By understanding the mechanics behind these platforms and recognizing their own emotional responses, children can develop a healthier relationship with social media that bolsters rather than detracts from their well-being.

Social media doesn't have to be an inevitable source of anxiety. When approached mindfully, it can be a source of connection, inspiration, and learning. Encouraging young people to curate their feeds intentionally, follow accounts that promote positivity and creativity, and engage in respectful digital dialogue are all steps toward utilizing social media as an uplifting tool. At the same time, it's vital for them to be reminded of the importance of face-to-face interactions and the depth of real-world friendships.

There's no denying the pervasive role that social media plays in the lives of young people today. But by adopting strategies to effectively manage its impact, these platforms don't have to become stumbling blocks in their journey towards mental well-being. Through guidance and support, parents and caregivers can nurture resilience in children and adolescents, equipping them with the skills to navigate the digital landscape confidently.

Ultimately, embracing the positive aspects of social media while maintaining vigilance over its potential harms can allow young individuals to flourish in their digital and physical communities. By fostering awareness and balance, we can help nurture a generation that thrives both online and offline, paving the way for a future where social media enhances rather than hinders their emotional and mental well-being.

Setting Healthy Boundaries

In an era where technology is inextricably woven into everyday life, setting healthy boundaries becomes crucial—especially for children and adolescents who are particularly susceptible to the alluring pull of screens. While technology offers remarkable opportunities for learning and connection, it can also be a catalyst for anxiety when not managed effectively. Establishing boundaries around technology use is not just an act of restriction but a proactive measure for nurturing well-being and resilience in young minds.

When considering boundaries, it's important to engage in open dialogue with children. Ask them how different digital interactions make them feel and encourage them to articulate both positive and negative experiences. Understanding their emotional responses can offer insights into where boundaries may be beneficial. It also sets the precedent that these decisions are collaborative rather than authoritarian, fostering trust and mutual respect.

One effective boundary is creating tech-free zones or times— periods or spaces where devices are off-limits. This might include family meal times, the hour before bedtime, or specific rooms like the dining area. These boundaries aren't just about limiting screen time; they are about promoting engagement in face-to-face interactions, reflection, and rest. Such breaks help reduce overstimulation and give the brain a chance to unwind, potentially alleviating some of the anxiety associated with constant digital engagement.

For parents and caregivers, modeling healthy technology use is equally important. When adults demonstrate balanced tech habits, children are likely to mimic these behaviors. This could mean intentionally placing your phone away during conversations or prioritizing outdoor activities over screen-based entertainment. Being intentional about technology usage shows young people that while screens are a part of life, they do not have to dominate it.

Establishing clear expectations about online behavior is another key aspect of setting healthy boundaries. Discuss the purpose of various apps and the appropriateness of different types of content. Conversations could center on what's acceptable in terms of communication with friends, engagement on social media platforms, and even the kinds of games played. Reinforcing the idea that digital footprints are real and lasting can urge young minds to pause and consider their actions online.

Schools can play a supportive role by reinforcing the digital boundaries set at home. By promoting a balanced approach to technology within educational mediums, they can set guidelines that help maintain focus and reduce anxiety among students. This collaboration between homes and schools creates a consistent framework that young people can depend on and navigate confidently.

Monitoring the effects of technology on a child's overall demeanor and mood offers actionable insights into how boundaries are working. If technology use seems to coincide with increased irritability or withdrawal from social interactions, it might be time to reassess and tighten the boundaries. This ongoing feedback loop ensures that any set limits remain relevant and effective as the child grows and technology evolves.

Importantly, empowering young people to set their own boundaries can be transformative. Encouraging them to recognize when a digital break is needed fosters self-awareness and self-regulation. This not only helps them manage anxiety but also prepares them for a future where they'll need to make these decisions independently. Providing them with the agency to define their limits builds confidence and allows them to practice autonomy in a safe context.

Technology is here to stay, and its integration into life is only going to expand. Thus, learning to draw the line where technology ends, and real-life experiences begin is essential. Well-defined boundaries act as an anchor, balancing technology use with activities that nurture the mind and body. Through thoughtful discussion, consistent modeling, and empowering young people to take ownership of their digital habits, we can help them build a healthier, anxiety-resilient relationship with technology.

Chapter 12:
Nutrition and Physical Activity

The connection between what we eat, how we move, and our emotional state can't be overstated, especially when it comes to managing anxiety in young people. Fueling the body with nutritious foods provides essential vitamins and minerals that support brain health and mood regulation. A balanced diet rich in fruits, vegetables, lean proteins, and whole grains helps stabilize blood sugar levels, which can significantly reduce anxiety symptoms. Meanwhile, physical activity acts as a natural stress reliever, releasing endorphins and promoting a sense of well-being. Encouraging children and teens to engage in regular exercise, whether it's a sport, dance, or a simple walk in the park, not only boosts physical health but also enhances emotional resilience. This synergy between nutrition and movement lays a foundation of strength and calmness, empowering young people to face life's challenges with greater confidence. By integrating these healthy habits into daily routines, families can create a nurturing environment that supports mental health and fosters a proactive approach to overcoming anxiety.

Eating for Emotional Well-being

In the maze of managing anxiety in youth, one often overlooked path is the impact of nutrition on emotional health. The food young people consume can play a crucial role in influencing their mood, energy levels, and overall emotional balance. Just as physical well-being hinges on what we eat, emotional well-being is equally sensitive to the choices made in the kitchen. By understanding the relationship between diet and emotions, parents and caregivers can empower children and adolescents to make mindful choices that bolster their resilience against anxiety.

Let's start by exploring the gut-brain connection. The gut, often dubbed the "second brain," is home to millions of neurons and an entire ecosystem of bacteria deeply connected to our brain. These microbes produce neurotransmitters like serotonin, which influence mood and behavior. When this balance is disrupted by poor eating habits, it can lead to increased feelings of anxiety and depression. Consequently, a diet rich in probiotics and whole foods can support a healthy gut flora, reducing emotional distress.

Aiming for a colorful plate is more than an aesthetic choice; it provides a spectrum of nutrients that support brain health. Vegetables like spinach and kale, berries such as blueberries and strawberries, and nuts like almonds and walnuts are packed with vitamins, minerals, and antioxidants that combat oxidative stress in the brain. Studies have shown that diets high in fruits and vegetables are linked to reduced symptoms of depression and anxiety in youth.

While incorporating these nutritional powerhouses can seem daunting, it doesn't have to be. Simple swaps can make a significant difference without overhauling the entire family menu. Consider exchanging sugary cereals for oatmeal topped with fresh fruit or blending leafy greens into a fruit smoothie. Involve children in the cooking process to pique their interest and encourage them to explore new flavors.

Besides the quest for balance in nutrients, sugar and caffeine are notorious culprits that can exacerbate anxiety symptoms. High sugar intake leads to rapid spikes and crashes in blood sugar levels, triggering mood swings and anxiety. Similarly, caffeine can increase heart rate and mimic or worsen anxious feelings. Limiting these can be key in maintaining emotional stability. Set boundaries around caffeinated drinks and sugary snacks, but also model this behavior as caregivers— what you eat leaves an impression.

Mindful eating is another valuable practice to integrate within families. It involves paying full attention to the experience of eating and savoring each bite without distractions. Mindful eating encourages slowing down and tuning into the body's hunger signals, which can help regulate eating patterns and improve mood awareness. Developing these habits early equips young people with lifelong tools for emotional management.

It's also important to address emotional eating—a coping mechanism many young individuals with anxiety rely on. Reaching for comfort foods in times of stress can form unhealthy patterns. While a comforting treat occasionally isn't harmful, becoming a regular crutch for distress is counterproductive. Help adolescents identify emotional triggers and direct them towards healthier coping strategies, such as engaging in a favorite activity or practicing deep breathing techniques.

Hydration, too, plays its part in maintaining emotional equilibrium. Dehydration can lead to symptoms resembling anxiety, like irritability or difficulty concentrating. Encourage frequent water consumption and make it a routine part of the day. Carrying a reusable water bottle can serve as a tangible reminder to stay hydrated, especially when kids are on the go.

For families searching for additional support, consulting with a nutritionist or dietitian can provide personalized guidance. These professionals can help tailor dietary plans that align with the specific needs and preferences of young individuals, making it easier to adopt and sustain healthier eating habits. A collaborative effort between medical professionals and families fosters an environment where children feel supported in their journey toward emotional well-being.

While nutrition alone isn't a silver bullet for anxiety, it is a vital component of a holistic approach to mental health. By intentionally choosing the foods that enter our bodies, we equip ourselves with the building blocks needed to combat anxiety. Empowering young individuals to make conscious nutritional choices not only uplifts their emotional state but also reinforces their agency over their wellbeing.

In shaping a future where young people are resilient and centered, food is an ally they can rely upon. The journey towards emotional wellbeing is as much about the mind as it is the body, and nurturing both through thoughtful nutrition lays a foundation for a more balanced life. As we conclude this section, carry forward the understanding that each meal is a decision, and these decisions weave the fabric of emotional health.

Exercise as a Stress Reliever

In the realm of managing anxiety, the spotlight often shines on therapies and medications, but there's a natural, often underestimated antidote that's available to nearly everyone: exercise. Engaging in physical activity isn't just about building muscles or losing weight; it's about reshaping the landscape of the mind. For young individuals and their caregivers grappling with anxiety, exercise can serve as a powerful stress reliever, bridging the gap between tension and tranquility.

Exercise has a way of reconnecting us with the present moment, much like mindfulness practices. The rhythm of running, the flow of yoga, or the concentration required in a game of basketball draws attention away from worries. In those moments, the mind isn't ruminating over past mistakes or future what-ifs. Instead, it's anchored in the here and now. This shift is crucial for young people who might otherwise find themselves ensnared by the endless loop of anxious thoughts.

But what makes exercise such a potent tool against anxiety? Scientifically speaking, engaging in physical activity leads to the release of endorphins. These natural mood lifters can provide a profound sense of well-being. After a session of heart-pumping activities, isn't it fascinating how problems seem a bit smaller, more manageable? That's the endorphins at work, combined with the sense of accomplishment after completing a challenging workout.

Some studies suggest that regular exercise can also help rebalance neurochemicals in the brain which are often imbalanced in individuals with anxiety disorders. For example, exercise increases the levels of serotonin and dopamine, neurotransmitters known for enhancing mood and feelings of pleasure. It's not just about the short-term rush; sustained physical activity can lead to lasting changes in brain chemistry, effectively lowering the baseline levels of stress and anxiety.

Introducing exercise as a stress reliever doesn't require a seismic lifestyle change. Small tweaks can blend movement seamlessly into daily routines. Consider starting with brisk walks. A walk in the park isn't just about moving the legs; it's about engaging all senses. Encourage your child to notice the rustling leaves, the crispness in the air, or even the distant drone of an airplane. This type of exercise combines physical movement with mindfulness, creating a dual approach that combats anxiety.

Variety and enjoyment are critical. If a child is passionate about music, perhaps dance could be a way to merge interests. If there's an affinity for nature, hiking could become a weekend tradition. Young people need to find something they love, something they'll look forward to doing, as enjoyment fosters consistency.

Let's also talk about the power of routine. Establishing regular exercise rituals can offer children a sense of reliability and predictability—an important counterbalance to the chaos anxiety can bring. Whether it's a daily jog with a parent, a weekly swim, or a

Saturday morning soccer match, these routines can form a comforting framework for both young people and their caregivers.

Beyond the physiological and mental benefits, exercise can serve as a catalyst for social interaction. Joining a team sport or a group class provides not just the opportunity to move, but also fosters connections with others. The shared goals, mutual encouragement, and oftentimes, laughter, can break through feelings of isolation. It's a reminder that they are part of a community, a powerful aspect when facing the trials of anxiety.

Parents and caregivers can play a pivotal role in normalizing physical activity by leading by example. When children see adults prioritizing exercise as part of their self-care routine, it underscores its value. It turns exercise from a chore into something that's embedded in daily life, helping young minds understand and internalize that caring for their physical self is integral to their emotional and mental well-being.

The goal isn't perfection. It's about progress, adaptability, and finding what works best for each individual. Listen to your child's preferences and explore different activities together. Encourage perseverance through challenges but ensure it stays fun and uplifting. Not every day will be easy, and it's essential to celebrate small victories along the way, as these moments lay the foundation for long-term resilience against anxiety.

Exercise as a stress reliever isn't just a section in a chapter. It's a powerful tool, a lifelong strategy. Encouraging this habit in young people today plants seeds for a healthier, more balanced future. One step, one jump, one game at a time, physical activity is an invitation to find peace and joy, even in a world that can feel, at times, overwhelming.

Chapter 13:
Sleep and Relaxation

In the chase for a peaceful mind, sleep and relaxation hold the key to unlocking a world of calm for anxious children and adolescents. Imagine bedtime as a sanctuary, where gentle routines—like a soothing story or a warm bath—usher in serenity. These rituals don't just prepare the body for rest; they signal to the brain that it's time to unwind. When woven with techniques for deep relaxation, such as guided imagery or progressive muscle relaxation, the impact multiplies. Young minds learn to gently slow their racing thoughts and embrace a sense of calm. As caregivers, the role is to cultivate this oasis by creating an environment free of arousing distractions, perhaps swapping screentime for a quiet moment of reflection. For anxious hearts, consistent sleep rituals—anchored in warmth and reassurance—can transform the daunting night into a realm of respite, building resilience with each peaceful night. It's through these woven threads of relaxation that both mind and body find equilibrium, setting the stage for confident, anxiety-free futures.

Establishing Bedtime Routines

As we delve into the daily fabric of managing anxiety, establishing a bedtime routine serves as a crucial thread. Sleep, as understudied and unglamorous as it may seem, is a powerful ally when tackling anxiety in young minds. It provides a foundation for emotional stability and resilience, offering young people the rest they need to face their fears with renewed strength. Yet, achieving a restful night is often more challenging than simply commanding a child to "go to sleep." It requires careful crafting of habits and environments that speak to both the heart and mind.

Children thrive on predictability and consistency, two cornerstones of effective bedtime routines. When a child knows what to expect, it reduces anxiety about the unknowns of the day. A successful bedtime routine isn't just about ensuring enough hours of sleep; it's about creating a sanctuary that envelops a child with calm and security. Consider introducing steps that guide them gently away from the day's worries—a ritual as simple as a warm bath, followed by a cozy read-aloud session can powerfully indicate that it's time to wind down.

Creating such routines might sound straightforward, but the challenge often lies in maintaining them amidst life's unpredictability. Here, consistency is your best friend. While flexibility is critical in other aspects of life, the boundaries you set around bedtime should remain firm. This doesn't mean being rigid; rather, it means being reliable. Establish some non-negotiable steps within the routine that can remain constant, even if the timing shifts slightly due to life's little surprises.

Take, for instance, the role of environment. The bedroom should be a haven—a place where anxiety holds no power. This is where the science of sleep hygiene intersects with the art of parenting. Keeping screens out of the bedroom is a common advisory, yet it can be a battle of wills with children attached to their digital companions. Here, inspiration and compromise come into play. Explain how screens can trick our minds into staying alert, and propose creative alternatives like audio stories or calming music to replace screen time before bed.

Another powerful part of a bedtime routine is nurturing a child's sense of control. Anxiety can often stem from feeling overwhelmed by circumstances beyond one's reach. By involving children in the creation of their own routines, you empower them to take charge of their well-being. Let them choose their book, their pajamas, or even the scent of their pillow spray. Small decisions like these teach them that they have agency, which can be extraordinarily comforting.

Don't underestimate the power of physical comfort. The bedding, room temperature, and even lighting can significantly alter how ready a body is to surrender to sleep. Soft lighting mimics the setting sun, signaling to the body that it's time to start the gradual descent into rest. Encourage the use of weighted blankets or fluffy duvets to provide gentle pressure reminiscent of a comforting hug. All these nuances work together to forge an environment that envelops a child in warmth and safety.

Furthermore, as bedtime approaches, it is crucial to be mindful of the emotional temperature of the household. Children are adept at picking up on familial tension, which can spike their anxiety right when they should be unwinding. Take a few minutes before bed to check in with their feelings. Use this time to discuss any lingering worries from the day. But remember, this isn't the time for solutions; it's a time for listening and validating feelings. You might find it helpful to introduce a simple breathing exercise to close out this ritual, creating a final bridge between the day and the tranquility of sleep.

For older children and adolescents, transitioning them into sleep might involve a part of the day called a "digital sunset." A gradual reduction in screen time as night approaches aligns with the body's natural circadian rhythms. Encourage practices such as gratitude journaling or guided relaxation to replace evening screen engagement. They provide an outlet for reflection and relaxation, steering the mind away from anxious thoughts that might fester unchecked in the quiet of the night.

One potential obstacle to establishing bedtime routines can be resistance, often a manifestation of underlying anxieties themselves. Here, empathy is key. Rather than viewing these moments as battles to be won, see them as opportunities to understand your child's deeper fears or needs. Work together to adjust the routine, if necessary. There's a balance to be found between discipline and understanding, and it often lies in gentle but firm negotiation.

In crafting these routines, never forget the role of modeling. Children learn more from what they see than what they're told. Show them how you unwind, how you respect your own need for rest. Share with them the rituals that help you transition from day to night, and discuss the importance of sleep for emotional and mental strength. Your actions will speak volumes, teaching them that peace and rest are not just aspirations, but essential destinations.

To conclude, establishing effective bedtime routines is less about following a strict schedule and more about building a nightly narrative that nurtures peace. It's the subtle symphony of preparation, environment, and emotion that sways a child gently into the arms of sleep. By investing time and thought into these routines, you're not only reducing anxiety but also crafting a legacy of restful resilience. As these nighttime habits mature, children learn to embrace sleep as a safe harbor, invaluable in their journey to managing anxiety.

Techniques for Deep Relaxation

In today's fast-paced world, finding a way to truly relax can seem like an elusive goal, especially for young people dealing with anxiety. The mind races, heartbeats quicken, and before you know it, a simple worry spirals into a full-blown anxiety attack. Teaching our children how to relax deeply is not just a luxury, but a necessity. With the right techniques, they can learn to manage their stress levels, gain control over their anxious thoughts, and rest both their bodies and minds.

First, let's delve into the calming magic of progressive muscle relaxation (PMR). This technique is all about tuning into your body and systematically tensing and then relaxing each muscle group. It's a wonderful practice for kids because it helps them become more aware of physical tension, which they might not even realize they're holding. Imagine starting at the feet and gradually working your way up to the top of the head, creating a wave of relaxation that travels throughout the entire body. Kids often find this method soothing, likening the release of tension to letting go of a clenched fist after holding it too long.

Guided imagery is another powerful approach. Also known as visualization, it involves creating a mental scene that's calm and peaceful. For children, this might mean imagining themselves in a favorite place, like a tranquil beach or a quiet forest. You might guide them through imagining the feeling of sand between their toes or the sound of leaves rustling. Engaging their senses in these mental images can block out the external noise contributing to their anxiety and transport them to a safe, serene mental space.

Breathing exercises are a cornerstone of deep relaxation techniques. Teaching children how to control their breath gives them a powerful tool to use during stressful moments. Techniques like 4-7-8 breathing can be particularly effective. It involves inhaling quietly through the nose to a mental count of four, holding the breath for a seven count, and exhaling completely through the mouth to a count of eight. This practice can slow the heart rate and calm the mind within minutes. The rhythm serves as a distraction from the spiral of anxious thoughts, helping anchor the child in the present moment.

Another technique that works well is the use of meditation, specifically designed for young minds. Meditation doesn't always mean sitting still in silence; it can be introduced through mindful activities such as walking or coloring. Encouraging children to focus entirely on the task at hand—whether it's the sensation of their feet touching the ground with each step, or the feel of the crayon against the paper—can create meditative states that quiet the mind. This kind of active meditation can be particularly engaging for kids who have trouble sitting still.

A lesser-known but highly effective relaxation technique is the use of aroma. Aromatherapy involves using scents like lavender or chamomile, known for their calming properties. These can be used in diffusers, as essential oils, or even embedded in a plush toy to hold during stressful times. The sense of smell is powerful and directly linked to the brain's emotional centers, making this an effective relaxation strategy.

Finally, regular physical activity plays a crucial role in deep relaxation. Exercise is a natural stress reliever, and it can be as simple as taking a walk outside or dancing in the living room. Activities that include elements of self-expression, like yoga or tai chi, are particularly beneficial. They not only improve physical health but also enhance mental well-being by focusing the mind and encouraging deep, rhythmic breathing.

In each of these techniques, consistency is key. Just like any skill, learning to relax deeply requires practice. As parents or caregivers, encouraging regular practice, perhaps even making it part of the daily routine, can pay off immensely in reducing anxiety. The most important thing is helping children find which techniques work best for them, empowering them to use these tools independently whenever they begin to feel overwhelmed. With time and practice, they can learn to harness their inner calm, building resilience against the challenges life throws their way.

Chapter 14:
Transitioning Through Life Changes

Coping with change and uncertainty can feel like navigating through uncharted waters, yet it's an inevitable part of life. For children and adolescents, these transitions—whether moving to a new school, dealing with family dynamics, or experiencing personal growth—can often trigger anxiety. Helping young people build resilience during these times is crucial. Encourage them to view change as an opportunity for growth rather than something to fear. Establishing routines and maintaining open lines of communication provide a sense of stability and reassurance. As caregivers, showing empathy and understanding their challenges fosters a supportive environment. Encourage them to focus on their strengths, setting small, achievable goals that highlight progress over perfection. With guidance and support, young people can emerge from these transitions with a renewed sense of confidence and an enhanced ability to tackle future challenges. Embrace change not as an end, but as a stepping stone to new beginnings, empowering them to face life's uncertainties with courage and resilience.

Coping with Change and Uncertainty

Change is a constant in life, yet it can feel daunting and unpredictable, especially for children and adolescents who are still learning how to navigate the world. Uncertainty often tags along, casting shadows on how these changes will play out. For young minds, understanding and managing these emotions can be tricky. But, by adopting the right strategies, they can learn not only to cope but to thrive amidst life's transitions.

Consider a young child moving to a new school. The scenario is rife with potential anxieties: new teachers, making friends, different routines. It's natural for them to feel overwhelmed. However, it's important for parents and caregivers to recognize that while the initial fear of the unknown can stir up anxiety, it can also be a chance for growth and resilience. By approaching these changes with a mix of empathy and encouragement, caregivers can help young ones redefine their relationship with uncertainty.

So, how can caregivers aid a young individual through such changes? First, it's crucial to acknowledge their feelings. Validating their concerns doesn't mean feeding into them, but rather saying "I hear you, and it's okay to feel this way." Words of assurance provide a safe space for open dialogue, allowing children to express their fears without the worry of judgment. This mental openness is the bedrock of coping strategies that foster adaptability and strength. Engaging in such conversations regularly can open the door to discussing these uncertainties before they grow into something unmanageable.

Routine is another powerful tool. Though life changes may disrupt existing patterns, creating new routines provides a semblance of stability. This stability serves as an anchor, offering comfort amidst the turbulence. While a structured environment is necessary, it's equally important to maintain some flexibility to accommodate the inevitable surprises that come with transitions.

Building resilience is a cornerstone of navigating change effectively. Encourage young people to see challenges as stepping stones rather than barriers. When they face uncertainty, remind them that each obstacle presents an opportunity to learn and grow. Share fictional stories or real-life examples of characters overcoming similar struggles; these narratives can offer perspective and hope.

Moreover, help them set realistic expectations. Often, anxiety stems from the fear of not meeting self-imposed or external standards. Teaching them to strive for progress rather than perfection can alleviate an incredible amount of pressure. It's okay if things don't go as planned—every change comes with its ups and downs. Reframing mistakes as learning moments rather than failures can significantly change their outlook on life's unpredictability.

Practicing mindfulness can also equip young minds to handle change with grace. Mindfulness exercises, such as deep breathing or focusing on the present moment, can ground children when they feel anxious about what lies ahead. These techniques don't just offer immediate relief—they build long-term resilience against anxiety.

Equally important is understanding the role of caregivers in modeling how to handle change. Demonstrating calmness and positivity in the face of life's uncertainties shows young people that they too can face unknown circumstances with confidence. Parents and caregivers who practice open communication about their own experiences with change help demystify the process, showing that it's part of everyone's journey.

It's also beneficial to remind young people that asking for help is not a sign of weakness. Encourage them to reach out to peers, teachers, or family members when feeling overwhelmed. Building a supportive network ensures they don't feel alone in their struggles.

Lastly, celebrate their victories, no matter how small. Successfully navigating through a change, overcoming an anxiety hurdle, or simply expressing their feelings should be recognized and commemorated. These celebrations are affirmations of their progress and courage, reinforcing their ability to handle future uncertainties.

Facing change is an inevitable part of growing up, yet by instilling confidence and providing tools for effectively managing uncertainty, we help young people see beyond the fear. They gain an awareness that, despite the mobility of life, they have within them the capacity to move forward with strength and positivity. With these skills, they can transform anxiety into an opportunity for personal development.

Building Resilience

Transitioning through the myriad changes that life inevitably presents can be daunting, particularly for young minds trying to make sense of the world. But within every challenge lies an opportunity to build resilience—a critical skill that serves as an emotional buffer, enabling us to adapt and thrive despite adversities. For parents, caregivers, and young people themselves, the question often is: How can resilience truly be cultivated and strengthened?

Resilience is not a trait people are simply born with; it's more like a muscle that can be nurtured and developed over time. Just as regular physical exercise enhances strength and endurance, consistent emotional practice can bolster one's capacity to recover from setbacks. It's important to understand that resilience is not about avoiding life's difficulties. Instead, it's about encountering them, drawing on internal and external resources, and emerging stronger on the other side.

Building resilience in young people starts with fostering a strong sense of self-efficacy. This belief in one's ability to influence events and master challenges is fundamental. Activities that encourage setting and achieving goals, however small, can considerably enhance this sense of self-belief. When children and adolescents experience success, they begin to internalize the notion that they can effect change in their own lives. Parents and caregivers play a crucial role in this process. By encouraging autonomy and decision-making, they help young individuals realize they have agency.

Another cornerstone of resilience is maintaining a positive outlook. This doesn't imply ignoring the negative aspects of life but rather reorienting focus toward the positive aspects and potential solutions. The brain's natural tendency often gravitates towards threats and difficulties, a remnant of ancient survival mechanisms. Teaching young minds to notice and appreciate the good—whether it's through daily gratitude practices or savoring small joys—can shift their perspective and bolster their resilience.

Moreover, developing healthy relationships is a critical part of the resilience-building equation. Whether it's a strong family unit or supportive friendships, relational networks provide essential emotional backing during tough times. Regular, open communication ensures that young people know they're never alone, no matter what changes come their way. These relationships offer a secure base from which they can explore the world and take calculated risks, knowing they have a net to fall back on if needed.

Life changes often come unannounced and can be accompanied by confusion, anxiety, and fear. Yet, establishing a reliable routine can create a reassuring framework amid chaos. Parents and caregivers can help craft an environment that balances consistency with flexibility. While predictable routines create stability, teaching adaptability ensures that young people are not thrown off course when routines are disrupted.

One vital way to foster resilience is by re-framing failure as a learning opportunity. Encouraging reflection on what went wrong and identifying lessons learned transforms mistakes into stepping stones. This mindset shift can drastically reduce fear of trying new things, further facilitating a resilient mindset. Children and teens can then approach problems with a focus on personal growth rather than avoidance.

Stress management techniques also play an essential role in resilience. Practices like mindfulness and deep breathing enable young people to manage emotional responses effectively. These skills encourage a calm mind and clarity in the face of uncertainty. Over time, this nurtures an inner resilience that prevents them from becoming overwhelmed during significant life transitions.

It's crucial to recognize that resilience is not a static end goal but a dynamic and ongoing process. The more diverse the experiences and challenges that young people face, supported by solid coping tools, the more nuanced and resilient their sense of self becomes. Parents and caregivers who model resilience by showing how they cope with their own life transitions provide a powerful, living lesson. Their examples serve as blueprints for young people navigating similar challenges.

Incorporating these resilience-building blocks into daily life equips children and adolescents to handle the foreseeable—and unforeseeable—changes that will undoubtedly arise. While we can't smooth all the pathways our loved ones will walk, we can certainly prepare them to face those paths with confident and resilient strides. Let resilience be not just a response to adversity, but an ever-present foundation upon which they can build their lives. Embrace the messy beauty of life's transitions as opportunities for growth, and trust in the incredible capacity of young minds to adapt, persist, and flourish.

Chapter 15:
Handling Academic Pressure

As young people navigate the challenging landscape of academia, the weight of expectations can feel immense, often leading to anxiety that overshadows their innate potential. It's crucial they learn to set realistic goals, ones that honor their unique capabilities rather than conforming to external pressures. Encouraging young people to focus on personal growth rather than comparison can transform their academic journey into one of empowerment. For those struggling with test anxiety, simple yet effective strategies, like mindful breathing and positive visualization, can be transformative. Parents and caregivers play a pivotal role in this process by fostering an environment where effort is celebrated as much as achievement, emphasizing progress over perfection. By offering support and understanding, you're laying the groundwork for resilience, nurturing a mindset that embraces challenges as opportunities for growth. Ultimately, handling academic pressure isn't about removing obstacles, but equipping young people with the tools to meet them head-on, imbued with confidence and self-assurance.

Setting Realistic Goals

Academic pressure can feel overwhelming for many young people and their caregivers. It is important to remember that the key to handling this pressure effectively often lies in setting realistic goals. Goals provide direction and purpose, but when they're not set thoughtfully, they can become a source of stress and anxiety. By approaching goal-setting with a balanced perspective, we can transform it into a tool that boosts confidence and resilience.

The first step in setting realistic academic goals is understanding each child's unique strengths and needs. Children are not one-size-fits-all, and their goals shouldn't be either. It's crucial to acknowledge that academic success is not solely defined by grades. For some, it might be mastering a challenging concept, while for others, it might be engaging more confidently in class discussions. Encouraging children to identify their personal goals helps cultivate a sense of ownership and motivation.

Being specific about goals can make a tangible difference in how achievable they feel. A vague goal like "do better in math" can be daunting and hard to measure. Instead, breaking it down into actions like "spend 30 minutes each day reviewing math problems" provides a clear path forward. Specific goals are easier to tackle and can give children a concrete understanding of the steps needed to achieve them.

No plan should exist without flexibility. Life is unpredictable, and so is a child's journey through learning. Whether it's a sudden illness or an unexpected school event, these factors can easily throw students off balance. It is essential that goals allow for such changes without being a source of further stress. Teaching children the importance of adaptability helps them cope with unforeseen challenges in the learning process.

Balancing ambition with feasibility is another critical aspect of setting realistic goals. It's natural for children to aim high, but goals should also be attainable. Unrealistic goals can lead to disappointment and diminish self-esteem, whereas goals that are within reach can motivate and encourage continuous progress. Parents and caregivers should guide children by discussing what feels challenging but achievable, ensuring their goals stretch their abilities without overwhelming them.

Let's also focus on the significance of time management. Properly managing time can be instrumental in achieving academic goals. Encourage children to create a schedule that allocates time efficiently to their studies, hobbies, and rest. This helps them not only to work towards their academic goals but also to maintain a balanced lifestyle. Good time management skills can prevent last-minute cramming, which often leads to anxiety, and foster a sense of control over their studies.

It's important for caregivers to celebrate incremental successes. Recognizing small achievements can significantly reinforce a child's motivation and build confidence. Whether it's improving a test score or completing a reading list, acknowledging these victories can inspire children to keep pursuing their goals. Celebration doesn't have to be anything extravagant; even simple praise can have a profound impact.

Providing a support system is another aspect of facilitating goal achievement. Children often need encouragement and assistance to reach their academic aspirations. By offering help, whether through tutoring, mentoring, or simply being available to answer questions, caregivers can play a pivotal role in helping children work towards their goals. A supportive environment is invaluable in fostering resilience and perseverance.

Furthermore, let's instill an understanding of intrinsic versus extrinsic motivation. Intrinsic motivation, which comes from an interest or enjoyment in the task itself, can be more impactful than external rewards like grades or approval. Encouraging children to find subjects or topics they are genuinely interested in can transform their approach to learning. When they understand that learning can be enjoyable and fulfilling in its own right, it promotes a lifelong love of inquiry and achievement.

Finally, maintaining open communication about goals is fundamental. Regularly discussing aspirations, challenges, and progress helps ensure that goals remain relevant and aligned with the child's current abilities and interests. These conversations provide an opportunity to adjust goals as needed and reassure children that needing to redirect is a natural part of growth and learning.

In conclusion, setting realistic academic goals is an ongoing process that requires careful thought and flexibility. By understanding individual capabilities, encouraging specificity, balancing ambition with feasibility, managing time effectively, celebrating small successes, and providing steady support, we empower children to tackle academic challenges with confidence and resilience. It's not merely about achieving goals but also about nurturing a mindset that values growth and the joy of learning.

Managing Test Anxiety

Academic pressure is an inevitable part of young people's lives, and among its many facets, test anxiety looms large for many students. It's more than just nervousness—it's a specific form of anxiety that can paralyze and hinder performance. Managing test anxiety is about more than outperforming academically. It's about fostering a young person's overall well-being and sense of self-assurance.

Understanding test anxiety begins with recognizing its symptoms. Students may experience physical manifestations like headaches, stomachaches, or a racing heart. They might also exhibit emotional symptoms such as irritability or overwhelming worry. These reactions often surface in the days leading up to a test and can escalate right before or during the test itself. Identifying these symptoms is the first step in addressing and alleviating them.

Employing relaxation techniques can be highly effective in managing test anxiety. Techniques such as deep breathing, progressive muscle relaxation, and visualization can help students calm their minds and bodies. For instance, taking slow, deep breaths before and during an exam can reduce stress levels and increase focus. Progressive muscle relaxation involves tensing and then releasing different muscle groups, helping to alleviate physical tension associated with anxiety. Visualization, on the other hand, allows students to imagine a serene place or successful outcome, creating a mental escape from anxious thoughts.

Another powerful tool is cognitive restructuring. This involves changing negative thought patterns that contribute to anxiety. Students often engage in catastrophic thinking, such as fearing they'll fail the test or predicting they'll never achieve their goals. By identifying these thoughts and challenging them, students can reframe their mindset. Encouraging positive self-talk, like "I'm prepared" or "I can do this," can replace those negative thoughts and build confidence.

Preparation remains key in minimizing test anxiety. Encourage students to develop a study routine that includes reviewing material over time instead of cramming the night before. Break down larger tasks into manageable chunks, providing a clear path to follow as they prepare. Adequate preparation instills a sense of control, minimizing anxiety's unpredictable nature. Also, practice tests can be invaluable. They not only familiarize students with the test format but also help reinforce their knowledge, boosting confidence.

Moreover, creating a supportive environment at home and school is crucial. Parents and caregivers can encourage open discussions about tests, providing a listening ear without judgment. Teachers, too, play a role by creating a classroom atmosphere where asking questions and making mistakes is okay. When students feel supported, they're more likely to view tests as challenges rather than threats.

Diet and exercise shouldn't be overlooked. A balanced diet can affect mood and energy levels, helping maintain focus during exams.

Foods rich in omega-3 fatty acids, antioxidants, and fiber can fuel the brain and support emotional stability. Additionally, regular physical activity reduces stress and improves mood by releasing endorphins, the body's natural mood lifters. Encouraging students to partake in physical activities they enjoy can provide a healthy outlet for their stress.

Sleep is another fundamental factor in managing test anxiety. Lack of sleep can exacerbate anxiety, impair concentration, and cloud judgment. It's important for students to establish a regular sleep routine, aiming for 8 to 10 hours of sleep each night. Creating a calming bedtime ritual, such as reading or taking a warm bath, can signal the body that it's time to wind down.

Day-of-test strategies can also help combat anxiety. Remind students to arrive early to the test site to avoid last-minute panic. They should also bring all necessary materials, reducing the stress of feeling unprepared. Likewise, during the test, students should focus on one question at a time, allowing the brain to concentrate fully on the current task instead of jumping ahead.

It's also critical for students to learn how to move on from test disappointments. Resilience is built when students view setbacks as learning opportunities rather than defining failures. Helping young people dissect what went wrong and devise a plan for improvement empowers them to approach future tests with a growth mindset. Celebrate their efforts, not just their outcomes, reinforcing that worth isn't solely determined by test scores.

Lastly, in some cases, professional help may be necessary. If a student's test anxiety is severe and persistent, consulting a mental health professional can be beneficial. Therapists can employ evidence-based practices like Cognitive Behavioral Therapy (CBT) to guide students in managing their anxiety effectively.

Ultimately, managing test anxiety isn't just about performing well in school. It's about equipping young people with the skills and resilience they need to face challenges in all aspects of life. By providing support, fostering a positive environment, and teaching effective strategies, we help create a foundation for lifelong success and well-being.

Chapter 16:
Seeking Professional Help

While navigating anxiety alongside a young person, there comes a time when reaching out to a professional isn't just a choice but a crucial step towards healing. This decision doesn't imply that you've failed as a caregiver; rather, it signifies a profound commitment to their well-being, showcasing strength and wisdom. Recognizing when to make this choice can be empowering, as a trained therapist or counselor offers fresh perspectives and effective strategies tailored to your child's unique needs. Professional help provides a safe space for young minds to explore their feelings, which might be difficult to articulate at home. Pursuing therapy or counseling can demystify overwhelming emotions and foster resilience by teaching skills that last a lifetime. It's important to remember that each child's journey with anxiety is personal, and seeking outside support can enhance their support system, offering specialized techniques and resources to aid their path toward a serene and fulfilling future.

When to Consider Therapy

Recognizing when to seek outside help for anxiety in children and adolescents isn't always straightforward. Sometimes, anxiety symptoms can be confused with typical childhood behavior, or it may seem as though the child will outgrow their fears and worries. It's crucial to understand that while some level of anxiety is normal, persistent or intense anxiety might require professional intervention. Therapy can be a transformative experience for young people struggling with anxiety, providing them with the skills they need to navigate their emotions and challenges effectively.

One of the first indicators that therapy might be necessary is when anxiety begins to interfere with the child's daily life. If they are consistently avoiding activities they once enjoyed, experiencing continuous worry that they can't control, or if their academic performance is suffering due to anxiety, these are strong signals that professional help could be beneficial. Therapy sessions can provide a structured environment where children learn to express their feelings and manage them in healthy ways.

Frequent physical complaints, such as headaches or stomachaches, without any medical cause can also be a sign that therapy is needed. Children may not have the words to articulate their anxiety, and it often manifests physically. In these cases, a therapist can work with the child to uncover the underlying emotional issues, helping them connect their physical sensations to their emotional experiences. This understanding can be empowering, giving children the tools to communicate more effectively about their feelings.

Moreover, parents and caregivers might notice that despite their best efforts, their support isn't alleviating the child's anxiety. Every child is unique, and sometimes, the strategies that work for one may not work for another. A trained therapist can offer a fresh perspective and develop a tailored approach to tackle the child's specific anxieties. They can also provide parents with valuable insights and techniques to continue supporting their child outside of therapy sessions.

Another consideration for therapy is if the child is experiencing intense reactions to specific situations. For instance, if phobias or severe social anxiety are preventing them from engaging with the world, a specialized therapy, like cognitive-behavioral therapy (CBT), can be particularly effective. Through CBT, children learn to challenge their negative thoughts and gradually face their fears, leading to more positive interactions.

Significant life events, such as moving to a new home, changing schools, or experiencing family changes like divorce, can also be burdensome for a child. While some may adapt smoothly, others might find these transitions overwhelming. Therapy during such times can equip young individuals with coping mechanisms to deal with change and foster resilience in the face of uncertainty.

Importantly, therapy can be considered as a preventive measure, not just a reactive one. Introducing a child to therapeutic practices before anxiety becomes overwhelming can be a proactive step in maintaining their mental health. Early intervention has the potential to minimize future struggles, as it acclimatizes the child to expressing emotions and seeking help.

Additionally, teenagers often face unique challenges that can heighten their anxiety levels. From academic pressures to social dynamics, the adolescent years can feel like a rollercoaster. Therapy can serve as a safe haven where they can discuss their fears without judgment and find constructive ways to deal with the pressures of growing up. It's a chance for them to discover more about themselves and understand how to set healthy boundaries.

Sometimes, there's hesitation about seeking therapy due to stigma or fear of labeling a child. It's vital to reframe therapy as a productive, empowering process rather than a sign of weakness. Encouraging open discussions about mental health can normalize the idea of seeking help, paving the way for children to view therapy as a resource rather than a last resort.

Overall, the decision to seek therapy should be guided by what's best for the child, taking into account their specific needs and circumstances. Consulting with a mental health professional can clarify whether therapy is the right choice, and if so, what type of therapy would be most beneficial. Together, with the support of caregivers and professionals, children can learn that while anxiety might be a part of their story, it doesn't have to define their future.

Types of Professional Support

When anxiety's weight begins to affect a young person's health, relationships, or capacity to learn, it might be time to consider professional intervention. Understanding the different types of professional support available can be empowering. Let's explore the diverse options, each offering unique ways to help young minds navigate their pathways toward balance and well-being.

Therapists and counselors form the first line of professional support. They offer a safe environment for children and adolescents to express their emotions and worries. Therapy sessions can take various forms, such as individual counseling, where the focus is on one-on-one interactions that delve into personal thoughts and feelings. Alternatively, group therapy might be an option, which encourages shared experiences among peers who face similar challenges. Both avenues help in fostering a deeper understanding of anxiety and equip young ones with coping strategies to manage it effectively.

Some situations might call for specialist input—a domain where child psychologists and psychiatrists come into play. Unlike general therapists, these professionals focus specifically on children's and adolescents' mental health. They apply specialized techniques and tools to evaluate and treat anxiety disorders, identifying patterns that could contribute to ongoing distress. Child psychologists often use cognitive-behavioral therapy to challenge negative thought patterns, while psychiatrists can assess if medication could play a role in a holistic treatment plan.

Navigating educational settings is often another aspect that needs professional handling. School counselors serve as vital allies in this arena. They work within the educational system to provide support, liaising between parents, teachers, and students to create an accommodating learning environment. By addressing anxiety-related issues within the school context, they aim to reduce stressors that could hinder academic progress and social development.

Family therapy is yet another supportive structure, emphasizing the family's role in managing anxiety. By participating together, families can learn about the dynamics that may influence a young person's emotional state. This form of therapy encourages open communication and understanding among family members, helping to create a supportive home environment. It can also equip parents and siblings with skills to assist their loved ones effectively, ensuring that everyone's needs are considered and respected.

For those dealing with severe forms of anxiety, intensive outpatient programs might be more appropriate. These programs offer a structured yet flexible approach to treatment, allowing children and adolescents to receive intensive care while still maintaining their daily routines. They typically involve multiple therapy sessions each week, combining individual, group, and family therapy, ensuring a comprehensive treatment approach. Such programs are designed to reinforce coping mechanisms consistently, helping young people develop resilience over time.

Teletherapy has emerged as a modern alternative, especially pertinent in today's digital age. This format offers therapeutic support remotely, making therapy more accessible to those who might not have the means to travel or who feel more comfortable in a familiar setting. Teletherapy can break down geographical barriers and allow for flexibility in scheduling, making it easier for young people to receive the help they need without additional stress or pressure.

Support groups offer another layer of assistance, focusing on community-driven support. These groups connect children and adolescents with peers undergoing similar experiences, providing a sense of belonging and mutual understanding. Facilitated by a trained professional, support groups offer a platform for sharing struggles and victories in a judgment-free space. It's an opportunity for young people to see that they're not alone in their journey, fostering empathy and camaraderie.

Each type of professional support has its place and importance, tailored to fit individual needs and circumstances. The key is to remain open to exploring these avenues, understanding that seeking help is not a sign of weakness but rather a brave step towards healing and growth. Together, with the right support, young people and their caregivers can face anxiety with renewed confidence.

In this journey of discovery, remember that it's not just about managing anxiety but about empowering young minds to thrive despite their challenges. Professional support acts as a guide, helping them learn how to harness and channel their emotions into positive outcomes, ultimately setting the foundation for a resilient, fulfilling life.

Chapter 17:
Encouraging Self-Expression

Fostering self-expression plays a vital role in helping young people navigate the waters of anxiety, offering them an avenue to translate their internal experiences into tangible forms. Through creative outlets such as art, music, and writing, children can explore their emotions in a safe and non-judgmental space, allowing them to articulate feelings they might struggle to express otherwise. Journaling, for instance, serves as a therapeutic tool enabling them to process their thoughts and emotions at their own pace, uncovering insights about their anxieties. As they see their feelings taking shape on paper or canvas, a sense of autonomy blossoms, encouraging them to confront and understand their anxiety creatively. This practice not only provides relief but also reinforces that emotions, even those tied to anxiety, can serve as a source of inspiration and growth. By nurturing self-expression, caregivers empower children to build resilience, equipping them with lifelong skills to manage emotional challenges. As they learn to articulate their innermost thoughts, they gain confidence in their ability to influence the narrative of their own emotional journey.

Creative Outlets for Emotions

In a world that often feels overwhelming, especially for young minds grappling with anxiety, creative outlets can be a beacon of hope. They're not just passive activities but dynamic ways to channel emotions, offering both respite and expression. This section invites parents, caregivers, and young people into a vibrant space where emotions become colors, rhythms, and stories—a powerful antidote to anxiety.

Art stands out as a universal language, transcending words and providing a canvas for the surreal landscapes of our emotions. Whether it's the broad stroke of a brush on canvas or the delicate etching of a pencil on paper, creating art allows young people to express feelings they might struggle to articulate. Not every child will embark on a path to be the next Van Gogh, but the act of creating is valuable in itself. Each brushstroke or doodle is a step towards self-discovery, enabling young artists to understand and navigate their inner worlds.

Equally transformative is the realm of music. For some, strumming a guitar, tapping a drum, or singing at the top of their lungs can offer a tangible release for pent-up emotions. Music therapy has gained recognition as a tool for emotional healing, promoting not just creativity but also mental health. Engaging with music, whether through playing an instrument or simply listening and responding, fosters an emotional connection and can alleviate anxiety. It nurtures an atmosphere where emotions can rise and fall naturally, akin to the rhythms of life itself.

Writing is another powerful medium through which emotions can flow. In journals, the chaos of thoughts and feelings can be transformed into coherent narratives. Storytelling, poetry, or even writing a letter to oneself can be cathartic, offering perspective and clarity. Writing provides a safe space where emotions are valid and acknowledged, fostering a sense of identity and understanding. Encouraging young people to write without fear of judgment can significantly impact their ability to process anxiety and express their emotions constructively.

Let's not overlook the power of dance and movement. Movement, in its many forms, releases endorphins, our natural mood lifters. Dance offers a physical outlet for emotions, whether joyful or solemn, allowing the body to express what words cannot. Encouraging kids to engage in movement, whether structured like ballet or uninhibited like contemporary dance, provides them with a non-verbal form of communication. It connects them to their bodies and can improve their self-esteem, balance, and coordination while reducing stress and anxiety.

For some, creativity blooms in the kitchen. Cooking and baking can serve as sensory experiences that ground young people in the present moment. The sizzle of onions in a pan, the tactile sensation of kneading dough, and the enticing aroma of freshly baked cookies can bring a sense of control and accomplishment. Sharing these creations with family or friends not only fosters a sense of community but also provides opportunities for appreciation and gratitude.

Gardening offers yet another avenue for creative expression, nurturing not only plants but also emotional well-being. The act of cultivating a garden can symbolize the nurturing of one's own mental health. Watching a seed grow into a beautiful plant mirrors the growth individuals undergo as they manage their anxiety. The patience and commitment required for gardening can teach young people valuable lessons about dedication and resilience.

Photography can be a window into the world, allowing young individuals to capture and frame their perspective creatively. With just a camera or even a smartphone, they can explore their environment, seeing beauty in what might seem mundane. Photography helps develop mindfulness, encouraging them to be present and fully engaged in the moment. This active engagement with their surroundings can provide a sense of calm and clarity amidst the chaos of anxiety.

It's essential, however, for caregivers and parents to support these explorations without imposing expectations. The goal isn't to produce masterpieces but to enjoy the process and acknowledge the emotions that surface along the way. It's about finding joy in the journey of self-expression and taking pride in the unique voice each person brings to the table, regardless of technical skill or artistic flair.

Recognizing the therapeutic potential of creative activities and encouraging kids to delve into a variety of artistic endeavors will equip them with a toolkit for managing anxiety. These activities not only foster creativity but also build resilience by allowing young minds to explore, express, and ultimately understand their emotions. This journey of self-expression, supported and nurtured, lays the groundwork for lifelong emotional health, helping kids transition from anxiety to empowerment.

Through embracing creative outlets, families can embark on a shared journey of discovery. Encouraging creativity doesn't just help manage anxiety—it's a celebration of individuality and the power of emotions. Together, these activities create a tapestry where each expression joins with others, forming a richer, more vibrant life story. These expressive endeavors, varied and personal, shine a light on the path toward mental wellness and emotional freedom.

Journaling as Therapy

In the landscape of anxiety management, journaling stands out as a remarkably powerful tool, inviting young people to explore their own minds and emotions. It serves as an intimate dialogue with oneself, a private space where true feelings can be expressed and sorted through without the fear of judgment. The act of writing transforms thoughts and emotions into tangible words, providing clarity and understanding. This can be especially beneficial for children and adolescents who often grapple with the nebulous nature of anxiety.

For many young individuals, pinning down exactly how they feel is one of the first challenges in dealing with anxiety. Journaling offers a way to sift through the clutter in their minds. By writing down their thoughts, children and teens are able to identify stressors and recognize patterns or triggers that may not have been apparent before. This simple practice can turn confusion into tangible awareness.

But journaling isn't just about identifying negative emotions. It also provides a canvas for self-expression, where creative ideas and positive experiences can come to life. Writing about achievements, hopes, dreams, and even daydreams, can bolster a young person's sense of self-worth and support their mental health. Encouraging children to write about not just what's troubling them, but also what excites them, can foster positivity amidst their struggles.

It's important to note that there's no right or wrong way to journal. This is a personal process, and its beauty lies in its adaptability. Some might prefer structured journals with prompts, while others lean towards freewriting, pouring out whatever comes to mind. From morning reflections to evening gratitude lists, journaling can be tailored to fit seamlessly into any child's routine.

Consider the power of daily journaling for a young person facing school-related stress. By setting aside just a few minutes each evening to write about their day—both the ups and the downs—they're able to release pent-up emotions. Over time, the pages accumulate to form a powerful narrative of resilience and growth. This habitual practice can become a grounding ritual in their otherwise turbulent day.

Parents and caregivers play an integral role in supporting journaling as a therapeutic tool. Encouraging a child to start a journaling habit can make all the difference. This encouragement might include providing them with a special notebook or setting a shared time for journaling in a quiet, comforting space. The idea is to make the journal a safe haven, free from critique, where honesty is celebrated.

It's crucial, however, to respect a child's privacy in this process. Journals are often deeply personal—it's their sanctuary. Parents should honor this by not demanding to read the entries. Instead, they can open a dialogue about what the child is comfortable sharing. Asking general questions, like "How did journaling make you feel today?" can invite conversation without infringing on private reflections.

For caregivers seeking structured approaches, guided journal prompts can be a helpful resource. Prompts such as "Write about a time you felt anxious and what helped," offer a starting block, easing any anxiety related to the blank page. Over time, these prompts can evolve, encouraging more in-depth exploration of emotions and thoughts.

Journaling not only assists in navigating current anxieties but lays down a blueprint for emotional management throughout life. By learning at a young age to articulate feelings in written form, children develop a lasting tool for emotional regulation. This can be a cornerstone of lifelong resilience, providing comfort and clarity when faced with future uncertainties.

Moreover, journaling is versatile. As young writers grow, their journaling can take on new forms—poetry, storytelling, letter writing—all offering different perspectives and insights into one's internal world. Each approach allows them to experiment with expressing themselves, discovering the joy and relief that writing brings.

Beyond individual benefits, journaling can also be a communal experience. Encouraging children to attend group journaling workshops enables them to share their experiences and learn from others. In a supportive group, they might gain new insights into managing anxiety, reinforcing the communal aspect of healing and the shared human experience.

In conclusion, journaling as therapy is not simply about writing; it's about connection—connection with oneself, one's emotions, and the evolving journey of handling anxiety. For young people and their caregivers, it's a tool of transformative potential, offering pathways to self-discovery and healing. By opening a blank page, they open a new avenue for hope, resilience, and expression.

Chapter 18:
Building a Support Network

Having a sturdy support network can make a world of difference for children and adolescents facing anxiety. It's about weaving a fabric of caring relationships that will help them feel connected and understood. Friends, family, teachers, and community members all play crucial roles in this tapestry, offering different perspectives and forms of comfort and guidance. When youngsters aren't alone in their struggles, they can better cope with the ups and downs of life. Encouraging the development of genuine friendships, joining supportive community groups, or even participating in local clubs can open doors to new relationships and shared experiences. It's pivotal to guide young ones in identifying their allies—those people who can offer an empathetic ear or a helping hand. Thoughtful discussions about feelings and fears become easier and more natural within supportive circles. Building this network isn't just about having fun— it's about fostering resilience and bolstering the psychological and emotional fortitude they need to thrive. As caregivers and parents, nudging children gently but confidently into the embrace of community and shared support can lay the groundwork for lifelong network-building skills. This connectedness imbues them with the confidence to confront challenges and turn challenges into stories of triumph.

Importance of Friendship and Community

In the journey of understanding and managing anxiety in children and adolescents, the role of friendship and community can't be overstated. These connections are not just beneficial; they are vital. Friends and a supportive community offer a lifeline, providing a sense of belonging, acceptance, and emotional support. When young individuals find themselves navigating the turbulent waters of anxiety, having trusted friends and a strong community network can make all the difference.

Imagine a place where children feel safe enough to share their innermost fears without judgment. That's the potential power of community. It creates an environment where young people can express themselves freely, knowing that they won't be ostracized or ridiculed. In these settings, friendships develop that are characterized by mutual respect and understanding. This, in turn, helps reduce feelings of isolation that often accompany anxiety. It reminds them they aren't alone in their struggles, providing reassurance and a calming presence.

Forming friendships during childhood and adolescence fosters critical social skills and emotional intelligence. It teaches young people how to communicate, empathize, and navigate complex social dynamics. These skills are critical in managing anxiety because they enable children to reach out for help, articulate their needs, and build stronger support systems. Moreover, when a child sees others coping with similar challenges, it normalizes their experiences and feelings. Recognition that others face similar issues can be comforting and empowering, warding off the belief that they're battling alone.

The influence of a supportive community extends beyond emotional aspects; it also impacts physical health. Engaging with friends and participating in group activities can significantly lower stress levels and boost mood. Physical activities like group sports or dance classes introduce endorphins, which are natural stress-relievers.

Additionally, shared activities promote cooperation and a sense of accomplishment, enhancing self-esteem and reducing anxiety.

Communities also play a crucial role in providing accessible resources that cater to mental health. Local support groups and clubs tailored to young people dealing with anxiety can offer a structured environment for learning and sharing coping strategies. Schools, religious organizations, and neighborhood groups are often excellent starting points for discovering these resources. They promote awareness, dismantle stigma, and encourage a collective approach to mental well-being.

Moreover, friendships formed within these communities can act as a protective barrier against the negative impact of anxiety. Friends can help each other recognize the early symptoms of anxiety and motivate one another to apply healthy coping mechanisms. In scenarios where professional help is needed, friends within the community can serve as a bridge, encouraging one to take that initial step toward seeking therapy or counseling. They essentially become partners in healing, supporting each other through the process.

Beyond immediate anxiety relief, friendship and community play a formative role in building long-lasting resilience and confidence. Children learn to weather setbacks and disappointments, knowing they have a 'safety net' of peers who stand by them unconditionally. The encouragement and feedback gained from these interactions foster a growth mindset—an understanding that failures are part of the journey and that they are not definitive or insurmountable.

Furthermore, teaching young people the importance of being part of a community helps them cultivate a sense of purpose and responsibility. When children feel they are contributing to something greater than themselves, it nurtures a sense of fulfillment and significance. Community involvement equips them with the understanding that they can influence change, an empowering realization that can mitigate feelings of helplessness that often accompany anxiety.

Encouraging parents and caregivers to facilitate these interactions is vital as well. Whether by arranging playdates, participating in community-sponsored events, or enrolling children in extracurricular activities, facilitating opportunities for forming friendships and community involvement is key. It sends a clear message that they too are advocates of these strong support networks, further solidifying the foundation of trust and security for their children.

In recognizing the importance of friendship and community, we're not merely identifying a support system but rather providing children and adolescents with an invaluable toolset for life. When ingrained early, these networks teach young individuals about empathy, resilience, and courage. They prepare them not just to cope with anxiety but to thrive despite it, fostering mental wellness that endures into adulthood. In essence, they're not only building connections; they're building a future where they feel empowered to face challenges with confidence and hope.

Finding Support Groups

When navigating the turbulent waters of anxiety, finding a community that understands can be incredibly reassuring. Support groups offer a shared haven where individuals and families experiencing similar challenges can gather, share, and grow together. These groups create a sense of belonging that is vital, especially for young people who might feel isolated by their anxiety. The power of shared experience cannot be underestimated, as it helps to normalize feelings and provides a platform for learning from others who truly "get it."

For families and young individuals living with anxiety, support groups serve as a critical lifeline. While therapy and professional support are indispensable, the communal aspect that support groups offer fills a different need. They provide the emotional sustenance derived from knowing you are not alone. In these groups, anxiety isn't something to be embarrassed about; instead, it becomes a common thread that binds people together, offering solace and understanding.

Parents and caregivers, in particular, benefit immensely from these groups. Often, they may grapple with their own concerns and frustrations, feeling unprepared to deal with their child's anxiety. Meeting others in a similar situation can be eye-opening. Hearing from parents who have successfully navigated the tricky landscape of anxiety management can provide new perspectives and strategies. These interactions inject hope and add layers of wisdom drawn from firsthand experiences.

It's important to explore various types of support groups to find one that fits best with your needs and preferences. Some groups focus specifically on parental support, while others provide a space for young people themselves to express their thoughts and feelings. Similarly, there are groups tailored to specific types of anxiety, whether it's social anxiety, generalized anxiety disorder, or even anxiety related to school pressures. Each group's unique focus allows for more targeted discussions and support.

Finding the right support group is an essential process. Begin by considering the logistics—would an online group suit your lifestyle better than in-person meetings? Online groups offer flexibility and convenience, extending the reach of support to those who may live in remote areas or have tight schedules. They often provide the comfort of attending sessions from the safety of your own home, which can be especially beneficial for those with social anxiety.

Conversely, in-person groups offer the invaluable connection that comes from face-to-face interaction. The warmth of shared laughter, empathetic nods, and the palpable energy in the room can be healing in itself. Meeting in person builds bonds quickly and strongly, fostering a deeper sense of community and belonging. Physical gatherings may also incorporate additional resources, such as guest speakers who specialize in child psychology or resilience training workshops.

When seeking a support group, word-of-mouth recommendations can be very helpful. Talk to mental health professionals, school counselors, or local community centers. They often have information about reputable groups in your area or online. Additionally, organizations specializing in mental health, such as the Anxiety and Depression Association of America or local branches of NAMI, can provide listings and insights into appropriate groups.

The dynamic of a support group can greatly impact your experience. Some groups are led by trained facilitators or mental health professionals who guide discussions and provide therapeutic insights. This can ensure that the group remains focused and productive, maintaining a safe environment for vulnerability and growth. Other groups might adopt a peer-led model, where members take turns facilitating. This approach can foster equality and mutual respect, encouraging shared leadership and personal empowerment.

As you explore these groups, it's crucial to keep an open mind. No group is perfect, and it might take time to find one that resonates with you. When attending your first few meetings, observe and ask yourself how you feel during and after the session. Feeling a sense of relief, hope, or connection is an excellent sign that you've found a supportive fit. However, if you feel discomfort or pressure to participate beyond your comfort level, it might be worth trying another group.

In addition to the emotional support, these groups can catalyze social connections outside the meeting space. Many lifelong friendships are forged in these environments, creating a support network that extends beyond shared anxiety. Such networks are particularly beneficial for young people, who thrive on peer relationships and often find courage and inspiration from one another's journeys.

Support groups also facilitate the sharing of practical tools and strategies that might not be covered in therapy or written resources. This peer-driven exchange of 'life hacks' for managing anxiety can be incredibly resourceful. Members often share books, apps, or videos that have positively influenced their understanding and management of anxiety, contributing to everyone's toolkit.

For young individuals, being part of a group of peers facing similar challenges can validate their experiences and reduce the stigma associated with anxiety. These groups empower them to voice their struggles and successes, building communication skills that are vital in all areas of life. This sense of agency is crucial in developing resilience and confidence as they grow.

The journey through anxiety can often feel like a solitary one, but through a supportive group, the road becomes a shared expedition. Building connections in these spaces offers a unique blend of empathy, education, and encouragement. Finding the right support group can be transformative, not just for the individuals experiencing anxiety but also for their entire support system.

So, take heart and explore the multitude of options available. Embrace the healing power of community and know that in sharing your journey, you can also inspire and uplift others. Support groups are about collective courage, where each member plays a part in weaving the fabric of a supportive, understanding, and, ultimately, transformative community.

Chapter 19:
Teaching Problem-Solving Skills

As we delve into the heart of empowering young minds, teaching problem-solving skills emerges as a crucial pillar for fostering independence and resilience. This foundational skill helps children and adolescents navigate life's challenges by breaking problems down into manageable parts, weighing options, and making sound decisions. By guiding them to understand that mistakes aren't failures but rather opportunities for growth, we instill courage and curiosity. Encourage children to brainstorm ideas and consider multiple perspectives, fostering creativity and flexibility. When they learn to take ownership of their choices and trust their judgment, they build confidence that carries them through the varied circumstances life presents. Our role is to equip them with these skills, offering support and encouragement, while gradually stepping back so they feel the satisfaction of mastering their challenges. By developing strong problem-solving abilities, young people not only manage anxiety better but also lay a solid foundation for lifelong resilience.

Effective Decision-Making

Teaching effective decision-making is an essential component of problem-solving skills, especially for young people navigating the maze of potential life stressors. In today's fast-paced world, decision-making is not just about choosing between options; it's about evaluating, prioritizing, and sometimes, making difficult choices under pressure.

Being able to make decisions confidently can significantly reduce anxiety, as uncertainty and lack of control often fuel it. Strengthening this ability supports young people in managing their emotions and reactions, fostering resilience in the face of challenges.

At the heart of effective decision-making is the ability to recognize and understand the problem at hand. This involves developing the skill to break down complex issues into manageable parts. Children and adolescents can benefit from guidance in this area, learning how to ask the right questions to clarify the problem. Encouraging them to view problems as opportunities for growth rather than insurmountable obstacles can shift their perspective and bolster their problem-solving confidence.

One way to cultivate decision-making skills is through role-playing scenarios. This technique offers a safe space for young people to explore different outcomes and potential consequences of their choices without real-world repercussions. Role-playing can also help them practice empathy by understanding how different decisions might make others feel, paving the way for more socially-conscious decision-making.

A vital aspect of decision-making is weighing the pros and cons of different options. Teaching children and adolescents how to evaluate these factors involves guiding them in critical thinking. They need to assess the potential benefits and risks associated with each option, considering both immediate and long-term effects. Encouraging them to think about how their decisions align with their values and goals can lead to more thoughtful and deliberate choices.

It's important for caregivers to teach young people that not all decisions will lead to positive outcomes and that making mistakes is a natural part of the process. Mistakes offer valuable learning experiences, prompting reflection on what went wrong and how similar situations might be approached differently in the future. This reflection fosters adaptability and resilience, highlighting that effective decision-making is a skill developed over time through practice and learning.

Mindfulness can be a helpful tool in decision-making, enabling young people to pause and consider before reacting. The practice of mindfulness encourages staying present and attentive, which can prevent impulsive decisions driven by anxiety or stress. By cultivating a habit of taking a breath and assessing the situation calmly, young people can enhance their ability to make decisions with a clearer mind.

While autonomy in decision-making is critical, it's equally important for young people to feel comfortable seeking guidance when needed. Encouraging them to consult trusted adults or peers can provide additional perspectives and insights they may not have considered. This balance of independence and support helps them feel empowered yet secure in their decision-making processes.

To support effective decision-making, caregivers can model healthy decision-making behaviors themselves. Demonstrating how to navigate complex choices and explaining the reasoning behind decisions can provide valuable lessons to young observers. Furthermore, discussing both successful and challenging decisions openly can normalize the process of making and learning from decisions.

Lastly, implementing a structured approach to decision-making can be beneficial. A simple framework could involve defining the problem, exploring alternatives, considering consequences, making a decision, and reflecting on the outcome. This structured approach can guide young people through the process methodically, helping them develop a consistent strategy for approaching decisions.

In conclusion, teaching effective decision-making to young individuals is a journey that requires patience, support, and practice.

By fostering an environment where they can explore, make mistakes, and reflect, caregivers can equip children and adolescents with the tools they need to face life's challenges with confidence and resilience. This essential skill not only mitigates anxiety but also prepares them for future independence and success.

Learning from Mistakes

Every child inevitably faces situations where things don't go as planned. Mistakes happen, and it's crucial we don't see them as failures but as valuable learning opportunities. For young people, especially those dealing with anxiety, the fear of making mistakes can paralyze progress and stifle growth. It's essential to approach these moments with empathy and understanding, instilling a belief that mistakes are a part of life's journey rather than a halt in it.

One of the first steps to embracing mistakes positively is fostering an environment that encourages exploration and experimentation. When caregivers model an attitude that values learning over perfection, young people are more likely to develop resilience. They start seeing mistakes not as reflections of their self-worth but as stepping stones in the learning process. A nurturing environment allows children to ask questions, attempt new things, and even step outside their comfort zone without the looming fear of judgment.

Invariably, when children make mistakes, their initial reaction might be distress, embarrassment, or frustration. Recognizing and validating these feelings is vital. It helps children understand that such emotions are normal and temporary. Encourage them to talk through their feelings, allowing them to process what happened. This process not only addresses their immediate emotional response but also provides an opportunity to start thinking critically about what can be learned from the experience.

Reflective thinking plays a critical role in learning from mistakes. After the emotional dust has settled, guiding children to reflect on what led to the outcome is beneficial. Ask them questions like, "What do you think didn't go as planned?" or "How might you approach it differently next time?" This encourages them to think about their actions and decisions without casting blame on themselves or others. Reflection helps them distinguish between the action and the self, nurturing the understanding that making a mistake doesn't equate to personal failure.

Moreover, it's important to discuss the mistake within the context of a larger goal or purpose. When young people can see how overcoming a setback contributes to their broader ambitions, they're more motivated to pick themselves back up and try again. Highlighting stories of people they admire, who've faced similar challenges, can also provide encouragement and a sense of connection to others' experiences. These stories affirm that everyone, at some point, has stumbled yet found ways to rise again, turning mistakes into invaluable lessons.

Creating a culture of open communication within the family supports this learning process. Celebrate efforts and small successes along the way, reinforcing the idea that trying is more important than immediate success. When children feel supported in discussing their mistakes without the fear of punishment or severe consequences, they're more inclined to address them forthrightly rather than avoiding or hiding them. This openness leads to a healthier relationship with mistakes, viewing them as opportunities to grow rather than setbacks.

Problem-solving skills are honed when children are encouraged to brainstorm solutions and consider alternative strategies. Engage them in conversations about possible ways to rectify the situation or improve future attempts. By involving them in the problem-solving process, you're empowering them to take control of the narrative.

They slowly build confidence, realizing that they have the capability to influence future outcomes positively.

At times, mistakes can involve conflicts with others, which presents another layer of learning. Teaching children how to apologize sincerely and repair relationships is crucial. This includes understanding the impact of their actions on others, empathizing with others' feelings, and demonstrating a willingness to make amends. Such social-emotional skills are foundational in fostering healthy, respectful interactions as they grow.

We must also acknowledge the difference between mistakes made due to lack of understanding and those stemming from anxiety-driven decisions. Anxiety can cloud judgment, leading to choices that might not align with a child's values or desires. Here, the learning focus shifts towards recognizing anxiety's role in decision-making and developing strategies to manage it effectively, preventing it from becoming a barrier to personal growth.

Finally, normalizing the conversation around making mistakes and the emotions that accompany them can help de-stigmatize the experience. Use age-appropriate language and relatable examples from your own life to guide discussions. Share your own mistakes and what you learned, showing children that the journey of growth is lifelong and everyone is bound to face challenges.

Embracing and learning from mistakes is not just about correcting an error; it's about building resilience, enhancing problem-solving skills, and encouraging a growth mindset. When children learn to view mistakes as essential components of learning, they develop the courage to pursue their goals without fear of failure, setting the stage for lifelong resilience and success. Through patience, empathy, and supportive guidance, we can help young people navigate their journeys with confidence, turning every stumble into a step forward.

Chapter 20:
Self-Care for Caregivers

Being a caregiver involves juggling numerous responsibilities, often leaving little room for personal well-being. Yet, fostering resilience in young minds requires taking care of one's own mental and emotional health. Just as you encourage children to embrace mindfulness or creative expression, it's crucial to model these habits yourself. Prioritizing self-care isn't selfish—it's an essential part of managing stress and promoting a healthy, balanced life. Consider integrating small, nourishing activities into your routine, like mindful breathing or regular breaks, to recharge your own emotional batteries. By doing so, you not only enhance your well-being but also demonstrate the importance of self-love and resilience to the children in your care. Remember, your health is pivotal, both for your sake and for those you're nurturing to thrive despite their anxieties.

Managing Your Own Stress

As a caregiver, you pour your heart and soul into nurturing and supporting a young person through their journey of managing anxiety. It's a selfless role, but often, it can lead you to overlook your own well-being. At times, the stress you're experiencing may not only impact you but also the child you're caring for. Stress has a way of seeping into the energy around us, influencing our interactions and the way we approach challenges. So, managing your own stress isn't just a personal endeavor; it's a crucial element in creating a calm and supportive environment for everyone involved.

Recognizing the signs of stress is an important first step. Stress can manifest in numerous ways: headaches, trouble sleeping, irritability, or even emotional withdrawal. It's your body's way of signaling that it needs attention. You might think it's noble or necessary to push through these signals for the sake of others, but it's not sustainable. Taking a moment to pause and reflect on how you're truly feeling can be transformative. Allow yourself to acknowledge these feelings without guilt. Remember, you're setting an example for the children watching you; understanding and addressing your emotions shows them the importance of self-awareness.

One effective approach to managing stress is establishing a routine that includes regular self-care practices. This isn't about grand gestures or elaborate plans. Simple activities, like a quiet cup of tea in the morning, a walk in nature, or ten minutes of meditative breathing, can be remarkably grounding. These small acts of self-care aren't indulgences; they're essential tools for maintaining your resilience and peace of mind. By consistently making space for yourself, even amidst a hectic schedule, you're fortifying your capacity to provide care and support.

Balancing demands and setting healthy boundaries is another critical component. It's natural to want to be available for your child 24/7, but this can lead to burnout. Clear boundaries help delineate your role as a caregiver while respecting your personal needs. It might mean setting specific times to focus on work, family, and, importantly, yourself. Communication is key here; feel comfortable voicing your needs to others in your life. By doing so, you're not only alleviating your own stress but teaching the young ones in your care about the importance of respecting boundaries—a vital life skill.

Stress management also involves cultivating a support network. Isolation can magnify feelings of stress and make challenges feel insurmountable. Reach out to friends, family, or support groups. Sharing your experiences with those who understand or are in a similar situation can provide a much-needed perspective and emotional relief. It's comforting to know you're not alone. Additionally, social connections can offer practical solutions and encouragement, allowing you to step back, recharge, and return to your caregiving role with renewed vigor.

Sometimes, the weight of your emotions or stress might feel too heavy to manage alone, and that's okay. Seeking professional support is a proactive and powerful step. Therapy or counseling can provide you with tailored strategies to cope with stress and enhance your ability to provide care. A professional can offer insights and tools that perhaps you hadn't considered, helping you navigate through complex feelings and situations. Plus, it models healthy behavior for the young ones, demonstrating that asking for help is a strength, not a weakness.

Moreover, integrating mindfulness practices into your daily routine can be incredibly beneficial. Mindfulness helps in anchoring yourself in the present moment, reducing anxiety about what could be or what has been. Engaging in mindful activities, such as deep breathing exercises or focused attention on simple tasks, can defuse tension and promote a sense of calm. The beauty of mindfulness is its accessibility; it doesn't require special equipment or training, just a willingness to pause and breathe.

Physical activity is another powerful antidote to stress. Exercise doesn't have to mean hitting the gym for an hour; it can be as simple as a brisk walk around the block, dancing in your living room, or a stretch session. Physical movement releases endorphins, often referred to as "feel-good" hormones, which enhance your mood and energy levels.

It's a dual benefit: you're taking care of your body and your mind simultaneously, improving your overall well-being.

As you practice managing stress, remember to celebrate small victories along the way. Did you manage to carve out ten minutes for yourself today? Pat yourself on the back. Did you communicate your needs clearly to someone who supports you? That's an achievement. Progress in managing stress is not always about monumental changes; it's the accumulation of small, consistent actions that create lasting impact.

In closing, as you navigate your role as a caregiver, understanding the importance of managing your own stress can't be overstated. The strength and stability you cultivate within yourself have a ripple effect on those you care for. By prioritizing your own well-being, you're not taking away from your ability to support others; you're enhancing it. As you walk this path, may you find balance, peace, and the inspiration needed to continue nurturing the children in your care.

Role Modeling Healthy Habits

As caregivers, you're often the unsung heroes in the lives of young people, providing them with unwavering support and love. But amidst the whirlwind of responsibilities, have you ever paused to consider the example you're setting? Role modeling healthy habits is a pivotal aspect of self-care for caregivers, and it goes hand in hand with fostering resilience in children. When kids see positive behaviors mirrored in their caregivers, they learn that healthy living is not just encouraged but embodied.

Imagine this scenario: your child is observing you as you navigate the ups and downs of daily life. Whether it's how you handle stress or the way you find joy in small accomplishments, your actions speak volumes. Kids are natural mimics, and by witnessing you prioritize self-care, they're more likely to develop similar habits. Think of it like planting a seed; with care and attention, it grows into something beautiful and strong.

Let's delve into a key aspect of role modeling: consistency. It's not about being perfect or having it all together all the time. It's about showing up, even on days when you might feel far from your best. Consistency in your self-care routines conveys to children that these habits are a non-negotiable part of life. You're essentially teaching them that taking care of oneself is as crucial as taking care of others.

Consider how you manage stress. Do you resort to unhealthy coping mechanisms, or do you take a mindful approach? Children closely observe how you respond to challenging situations, and your strategies can become their learning tool. Demonstrating healthy stress management techniques, such as deep breathing or stepping outside for a walk, can profoundly influence their approach to anxiety.

Moreover, modeling a balanced lifestyle is central to instilling healthy habits. Balancing work, family, and personal time is challenging, yet showing that it's achievable can inspire young minds to strive for the same equilibrium. Engage in activities that replenish you—perhaps it's reading a good book, participating in a hobby, or simply enjoying quiet time.

Nutrition and physical activity are also essential components of role modeling. When children see you making nutritious food choices or witnessing your commitment to regular exercise, they're more inclined to adopt similar practices. Eating together as a family, when possible, is a perfect opportunity to demonstrate the enjoyment of nutritious meals. You don't need to be a gourmet chef; simple, healthy dishes can spark a lifelong relationship with good eating habits.

Let's touch on the importance of sleep and relaxation. Display the value of a good night's sleep by maintaining regular sleep schedules, even on weekends. Establishing a wind-down routine not only benefits you but serves as a visual cue for kids that sleep is a priority. This consistency can help stave off anxiety and foster well-being.

In addition to physical health, emotional well-being is paramount. Expressing emotions openly and appropriately shows children that it's okay to feel and talk about their feelings. When you're upset or frustrated, verbalizing these emotions in a constructive way provides a template for children to express themselves. This helps them understand that emotions aren't to be feared but managed healthily.

Interweaving self-care into everyday interactions is another powerful method of role modeling. For example, taking a moment to pause and practice gratitude before meals or reflecting on positive events of the day can cultivate mindfulness and appreciation in young ones. These small practices subtly reinforce the mindset that self-care and mindfulness should be interwoven into the fabric of everyday life.

Undoubtedly, there are moments when life feels overwhelming, and maintaining these habits can seem daunting. That's why it's crucial to acknowledge your own limitations and seek help when needed. Demonstrating the courage to ask for support from friends, family, or professionals is not a sign of weakness but of strength. It sets a precedent that it's perfectly acceptable to lean on others in times of need.

Ultimately, role modeling healthy habits is a journey, not a destination. It transcends simply adhering to a set of behaviors; it's about nurturing a climate of well-being within you and spreading its influence to those you care for. With mindfulness and intent, you can be the lighthouse that guides young minds towards a future where self-care and resilience stand at the helm.

As you continue this journey of self-discovery and growth, remember that your efforts as a caregiver resonate beyond the immediate. You're not just fostering healthy habits; you're creating a legacy of well-being that will ripple through generations. And that, without a doubt, is an inspiring pursuit.

Chapter 21:
Understanding Medication

Diving into the world of medication for anxiety can feel like a daunting journey, but it's important to understand it as one of several tools in your toolkit. When anxiety becomes overwhelming and other strategies aren't enough, medication might be considered to help bring relief and restore balance. It's crucial to weigh the potential benefits, such as reducing severe symptoms and improving your young one's ability to function and thrive, against possible side effects. Collaborating with experienced health professionals ensures that every decision is informed and tailored to your child's unique needs. Remember, medication isn't a standalone solution but rather a component of a comprehensive approach that includes therapy, support, and self-care. With the right understanding and approach, medication can play a valuable role in managing anxiety and fostering resilience.

When Medication May Be Needed

Deciding when medication might be an appropriate step can be a weighty decision for parents, caregivers, and young people. It's not a choice made lightly, nor should it be. Understanding the context and necessity of medication in managing anxiety requires careful consideration of many factors.

Anxiety, like any other mental health condition, exists on a spectrum. For some children and teens, anxiety is a transient phase linked to specific events or phases of life. For others, it's an overpowering force, infiltrating every corner of daily existence. When anxiety begins to disrupt school, relationships, and the joys of youth, it might be time to consider additional interventions. Medication is never about masking symptoms; it's about opening paths to healing and learning how to manage those overwhelming feelings effectively.

Before jumping to conclusions about medication, there needs to be a comprehensive evaluation. This involves collaboration with healthcare professionals who specialize in mental health, such as pediatricians, child psychologists, or psychiatrists. These professionals can help assess the severity of anxiety and the impact it's having on day-to-day life. Engaging with professionals can be reassuring for families; knowing you're not alone on this journey can alleviate some of the stress of decision-making.

Over the course of treatment, non-medication strategies, like therapy or lifestyle modifications, are often the first lines of defense. But sometimes they might not be enough on their own. When therapy, lifestyle changes, and support systems don't afford the relief needed, medication might be considered as a supplementary aid.

The decision to use medication can often be a turning point. For some, it's viewed with apprehension, raising concerns about side effects or the stigma attached to "needing medicine." Even still, it's important to recognize that just as some physical ailments require medication, so might psychological ones. A close understanding of what medication can achieve is crucial. It may not always eradicate anxiety completely, but it can make anxiety more manageable, creating space for children and their caregivers to focus on other therapeutic interventions and coping strategies.

An important aspect of this discussion is understanding the types of medication used in treating anxiety in young people. There are different classes of medication commonly used, such as selective serotonin reuptake inhibitors (SSRIs) and benzodiazepines, each with its unique action, benefits, and drawbacks. Generally, SSRIs are more commonly prescribed for long-term management, as they help adjust neurotransmitter levels to better manage anxiety as a chronic condition. Benzodiazepines, on the other hand, may be used for short-term relief due to their calming effects but can have issues such as dependency. The specific choice depends on individual needs and circumstances, and a healthcare professional can guide families toward the best approach.

Medication isn't a cure-all; it's not the end of the journey but a pivotal part of it. It's about building a foundation of stability that enables further progress through ongoing therapy and support. The intricate balance is found in using medication alongside therapies such as CBT, lifestyle adjustments, and the nurturing support of families and communities.

Parents and caregivers might worry about the implications of medication on long-term development, a valid concern that should be addressed openly with a healthcare provider. It's essential to weigh the pros and cons, considering the relief medication may offer against its potential side effects. Monitoring and adjusting the dosage as guided by professionals can aid in minimizing any adverse effects.

One of the most persuasive factors in deciding to use medication can often be the child's quality of life. If they are hindered from engaging in normal activities, forming friendships, or even attending school due to incapacitating anxiety, then medication becomes not just an option but a necessity for regaining normalcy and facilitating a happier, healthier life.

Medication, when combined with counseling and emotional support, becomes part of a comprehensive treatment plan designed for long-term success. Confidence in the process grows over time as children and their families see positive changes and gains in self-assurance. The journey is unique for each individual, and every step taken towards overcoming anxiety marks significant progress.

An open, ongoing conversation with healthcare providers is key throughout this process. Regular reviews and assessments ensure that medication continues to be the right choice and is administered at the most effective dose. This keeps caregivers informed and actively involved in the treatment, fostering a supportive environment for the child or adolescent.

Ultimately, the decision for a child or teen to start medication for anxiety should never be made in isolation. Discussion, research, and professional guidance combine to make the best choice for the child's future. The goal is support, empowerment, and enabling young minds to explore their world without inhibition or fear. The path to finding balance might include medication as a necessary ally, a partner in the ongoing journey towards resilience and freedom from anxiety's grasp.

Benefits and Side Effects

Understanding the role of medication in managing anxiety is a vital aspect of supporting your child or adolescent on their journey to well-being. When anxiety becomes overwhelming and seems to overpower other strategies like talk therapy or daily coping mechanisms, medication can sometimes offer relief. However, it's not a one-size-fits-all approach, and it's important to weigh the benefits against potential side effects.

One of the primary benefits of medication is its ability to quickly and effectively reduce severe anxiety symptoms, enabling a child to participate more fully in daily life and therapeutic activities. Medications such as selective serotonin reuptake inhibitors (SSRIs) can help balance chemicals in the brain, often leading to a more stable emotional state. This stability can open the door for young people to better engage in activities, perform in school, and develop healthier relationships.

Moreover, medication may provide the necessary foundation for other interventions to be more effective. When a child isn't overwhelmed by anxiety, they're more receptive to cognitive-behavioral techniques and can better implement mindfulness practices, fostering a comprehensive approach to managing their anxiety. It's like clearing the path for other tools to work effectively.

Despite these benefits, it's crucial to approach medication with informed caution due to its potential side effects. Some children and adolescents might experience nausea, fatigue, or changes in appetite. These side effects can contribute to hesitancy around medication, and it's important to discuss any concerns with a healthcare professional who can tailor a prescription that minimizes adverse effects while maximizing benefits.

The impact of medication is not solely physiological. It can also provide a psychological lift, instilling a sense of hope and possibility. For some young people, knowing there is a medical aid available can reduce the stigma around anxiety, encouraging them to view it as a manageable condition rather than a personal failing. This perspective shift can serve as a catalyst for growth and acceptance.

Open communication between the child, caregivers, and healthcare providers is essential when considering medication. This ensures that any decisions are made collaboratively, respecting the child's feelings and concerns. Involving them in discussions about their treatment plan can empower them, reinforcing the idea that they have control over their journey to feeling better.

Balancing the decision to use medication with other therapeutic strategies is key. Medication should not be viewed as a standalone solution but rather as part of a broader strategy that includes therapy, lifestyle changes, and support systems. It's a tool that, when used thoughtfully and deliberately, can significantly aid in managing anxiety.

Regular monitoring and check-ins with healthcare professionals are crucial to ensure that medication remains beneficial over time. As children grow and their symptoms potentially evolve, adjustments may be necessary. Being proactive about these adjustments can help in mitigating any new side effects and enhancing the overall success of the treatment plan.

Ultimately, while the decision to use medication can be daunting, understanding its possible benefits and side effects allows caregivers and young people to make informed, confident choices. The goal is always to find the right balance that supports a young person's growth and provides them with the best opportunity to lead a happy, resilient life.

Chapter 22:
Preventing Future Anxiety

As we look ahead, preventing future anxiety involves more than just reacting to present challenges; it's about laying a foundation that fosters resilience and adaptability in young minds. By instilling long-term coping skills, we equip children and adolescents with the tools they need to navigate life's unpredictable waters. Encouraging adaptability means nurturing a mindset that views change not as a threat but as an opportunity for growth and learning. It's crucial to integrate these skills into everyday routines and reinforce them through genuine support and encouragement. This nurturing process empowers young people to approach the future with confidence, knowing they have a robust toolkit to handle whatever comes their way. By actively engaging in this preventive mindset, parents and caregivers play a pivotal role in shaping a future where anxiety doesn't rule but rather serves as a stepping stone to resilience.

Instilling Long-Term Coping Skills

Building a sturdy foundation of long-term coping skills is essential for young people battling anxiety. It goes beyond just managing immediate symptoms—it's about equipping them with tools that can foster resilience throughout their lives. Imagine giving a young person a toolkit. They can pull out what they need, as they need it, to fix or even prevent anxiety-related scenarios. This approach not only empowers them but also instills confidence in their ability to handle the inevitable ups and downs of life.

One powerful step in instilling long-term coping skills is nurturing self-awareness. Self-awareness acts as a compass, guiding young people through the stormy seas of anxiety. When they understand what triggers their anxiety, they gain control and can actively choose how to respond. Encouraging regular reflection can be a simple yet effective method. Whether it's through journaling, art, or quiet contemplation, young minds can explore and become familiar with their emotional landscapes. This awareness allows them to anticipate challenges and prepare strategies to handle them, reducing the feeling of being overwhelmed.

Another crucial aspect is teaching adaptive thinking. How a child interprets challenging situations significantly affects their ability to cope. Introducing cognitive reframing techniques can be a game-changer. This technique involves recognizing irrational and negative thoughts and replacing them with balanced and realistic perspectives. For example, if a child fears presenting in class because they might make a mistake, help them see that everyone makes mistakes, and it's a part of learning. Over time, this shift in thinking helps build a more resilient and flexible mindset.

Moreover, instilling problem-solving skills enhances a child's ability to manage their anxiety. It's about moving from feeling stuck to feeling capable. Problem-solving doesn't just magically happen; it's a skill to be taught and honed. Start by encouraging young people to break large, intimidating problems into smaller, manageable parts. Then guide them through brainstorming potential solutions for each part. Celebrating small victories along the way adds a layer of positivity and encourages a proactive approach whenever they face new challenges. This approach not only addresses the issue at hand but also builds confidence in their problem-solving abilities.

Moreover, fostering emotional regulation strategies is vital. Emotions can be overwhelming, especially during a surge of anxiety. Techniques like deep breathing, mindfulness, and progressive muscle relaxation can be taught and practiced regularly. These methods help calm the body and mind, providing immediate relief and long-term benefits. As these practices become second nature, children and adolescents can draw on them in moments of stress, leading to greater emotional stability.

The support system also plays an invaluable role in this journey. Building a reliable network of friends, family, and mentors who can offer guidance and understanding can significantly boost a young person's ability to cope. These relationships provide not only emotional reinforcement but also practical advice in times of need. Encouraging young people to reach out and share their thoughts or seek support when they're struggling helps minimize the stigma often associated with anxiety. Knowing they aren't alone is a powerful tool unto itself.

Encouraging a sense of adaptability can also contribute to long-term coping. Life is unpredictable, and the ability to adapt to changes can lessen anxiety's impact. Engage children in activities that challenge their flexibility, like trying new hobbies or learning new skills. Adaptability helps them understand that while they can't control every event, they can control how they respond to it. This acceptance and willingness to grow in changing circumstances equip them with a robust set of coping skills that will serve them throughout their lives.

Importantly, instilling long-term coping skills involves positive reinforcement and celebration of effort rather than just outcomes. Evaluate progress not just by visible achievements but by recognizing the small yet crucial steps a young person takes towards managing their anxiety. Create an environment where effort and perseverance are honored, thereby fostering a growth mindset. This recognition inspires continued effort and reinforces the idea that resilience is built through persistence and practice.

Finally, aim to model these coping strategies in your daily interactions. Young minds are observant, often picking up and mimicking how adults handle stress and adversity. Demonstrating healthy coping mechanisms, showing patience and understanding when mistakes happen, and practicing self-care openly can provide a living blueprint for young people to follow. You become a living lesson, illustrating that it's possible to manage anxiety effectively and lead a fulfilling life.

Ultimately, the journey of instilling long-term coping skills is about creating a lifelong foundation of resilience. It's about teaching young people to weather the storms of anxiety with confidence and grace, armed with an arsenal of skills they can rely on for years to come. And while this journey doesn't offer quick fixes or magic solutions, it promises the opportunity for growth, understanding, and, most importantly, hope. As young people learn to balance their emotional lives, they unlock the potential to face the world with courage and resilience. In essence, they become architects of their own well-being.

Encouraging Adaptability

In our rapidly changing world, perhaps one of the most valuable skills we can encourage in young people is adaptability. This is not just about teaching them to react to change, but about fostering a mindset that thrives on it. For many children and adolescents, anxiety often stems from the unknown—the possibility of what might happen and the fear that they aren't equipped to handle it. When we encourage adaptability, we are preparing them not just to survive change, but to see it as an opportunity for growth and learning.

Adaptability starts with a shift in perspective. It involves viewing challenges and changes not as threats, but as chances to develop new skills and insights. This involves teaching children to be open-minded and flexible in their thinking. Instead of immediately reacting to new situations with fear or anxiety, we can guide them to pause and explore the possibilities these changes might bring. By framing change as an ally rather than an adversary, we begin to diminish the hold that anxiety has on their minds.

One practical way to inspire adaptability is through exposure to diverse experiences. Encourage children to engage in a variety of activities, even those outside their comfort zones. This diversity helps them learn to approach new situations with curiosity instead of hesitation. When they play a new sport, join a different club, or try their hand at art, they're not just gaining new knowledge—they are actively practicing adaptability. These experiences help create neural pathways in the brain that equip them to handle unforeseen circumstances both calmly and effectively.

Moreover, role modeling adaptability as parents or caregivers profoundly influences children's perceptions of change. When children witness adults responding to change with positivity and resilience, it sends a powerful message. It tells them that flexibility isn't just a survival skill—it's a path to success. Share stories of times when you've had to adapt and the skills you gained as a result. Highlight moments of difficulty that led to positive growth or lifelong interests. Every story you share adds another piece to the puzzle that is their understanding of adaptability.

In addition, the importance of maintaining a supportive, open environment cannot be overstated. Encourage young people to ask questions about things they don't understand. When they encounter changes or challenges, being able to talk about them without fear of judgment makes them more likely to process these emotions healthily. Discussing feelings and fears helps them realize that anxiety around change is normal, but it doesn't have to dictate their actions. An open dialogue helps them feel supported, no matter what they're facing.

Building adaptability is also about laying a foundation of resilience. Children should learn that it's okay to fail and that each failure is a stepping stone to success. Help them reframe failure not as a personal flaw, but as an invaluable learning experience. Encourage them to reflect on what went wrong and how they can approach the situation differently next time. This reflection instills a growth mindset, making anxiety less about the fear of failure and more about anticipation for growth.

It's also crucial to build decision-making skills. Equip children with the ability to make informed and thoughtful choices. Engaging them in small decisions in their daily lives gradually builds confidence for larger decisions. Discuss the pros and cons of different choices, and let them see the outcomes of their decisions. This process teaches them that they can handle unexpected results and adapt their plans as needed.

Challenges will inevitably arise, and when they do, practicing mindfulness can make a significant difference. Mindfulness trains the mind to live in the present, to face what is happening now rather than worrying about what could happen next. Techniques like mindful breathing or meditation can help halt the onset of anxiety at the root, leaving space for calm reflection rather than panic. Teach children that by anchoring themselves in the present, they not only manage anxiety better but also engage more fully with the possibilities of change.

Another component of fostering adaptability is preparing for future challenges through scenario planning. This doesn't mean dwelling on negative possibilities but rather practicing how one might respond to various scenarios. It can be as simple as asking, "What would we do if...?" This exercise isn't about planning for every possible outcome but about building confidence in one's ability to adapt. It reinforces the belief that they have the resources and resilience to handle whatever comes their way.

Adapting requires not only personal resilience but also social support. Encourage young people to build strong relationships with peers and mentors, who can provide perspective and advice in times of change. A supportive network acts as a buffer against the anxiety that uncertainty might bring. Participating in group activities or collaborative projects can help strengthen these bonds, providing them with a team to rely on in uncertain times.

When young people are encouraged to develop adaptability, they become capable not only of tackling today's changes but also of welcoming tomorrow's. They learn to embrace uncertainty as part of life, rather than something to be feared. This empowering journey through change ultimately positions them to lead lives full of exploration, growth, and newfound strength. It's through adaptability that anxiety loses its grip, making way for a future where challenges are but stepping stones to greater heights.

Chapter 23:
Celebrating Progress

In our journey through understanding and managing anxiety, celebrating progress is not just a delightful acknowledgment of achievements but a powerful catalyst that propels us toward continued growth. As we reflect on the milestones reached, both big and small, it becomes crucial to recognize how far we've come and acknowledge the bravery it takes to confront fears. This chapter illuminates the importance of pausing to honor victories—whether it's mastering a coping technique or overcoming a specific worry. By setting new goals, we lay the groundwork for continuous evolution, ensuring that progress isn't a destination but an ongoing journey. Encouragement, positive reinforcement, and applause for efforts made make resilience a living, breathing part of daily life. So, let's embrace every step forward, knowing that each one builds a foundation for overcoming future challenges, enhancing confidence, and nurturing the unwavering strength within young hearts. Progress, after all, is the heartbeat of transformation.

Recognizing and Rewarding Achievements

Celebrating progress in any form is an essential part of managing and overcoming anxiety. It's not just about reaching the end destination but acknowledging the small steps taken along the way. Recognizing and rewarding achievements can be a powerful tool in building confidence and resilience in children and adolescents who are grappling with anxiety. This approach fosters a sense of accomplishment and encourages further efforts, making the journey less daunting and more rewarding.

One of the best ways to recognize achievements is by identifying specific goals that the young person has set for themselves, even if they seem minor at first glance. Achievements can range from expressing their feelings in a supportive environment to trying out a new coping strategy. For instance, if a child manages to communicate their anxiety openly to a family member, that's a victory worth acknowledging. These small victories are foundational to building resilience and independence.

When rewarding these achievements, it's vital to ensure that the recognition is appropriate and meaningful. This doesn't always mean material rewards. In fact, often the most impactful acknowledgments are verbal affirmations or shared experiences. Simple phrases like "I'm proud of you" or "Look how far you've come" can work wonders in reinforcing positive behavior. Celebrating with a special outing, even just a walk in the park or an extra story at bedtime, can also reinforce the importance of their progress.

It's important to create an environment where children feel appreciated for their efforts without fear of judgment. This can be established by regularly sharing successes in a family setting. Perhaps at dinner, each family member shares something positive about their day. This practice not only reinforces individual achievements but also cultivates a supportive family atmosphere where everyone feels valued and acknowledged.

Recognizing achievements doesn't mean constantly praising every action. The aim is to encourage genuine efforts and progress. When children overcome specific anxiety-related challenges, it's an opportunity to highlight their courage and tenacity. This approach helps them understand that anxiety can be managed and that they have the strength to confront it. Over time, these acknowledgments foster a sense of empowerment that stays with children into adulthood.

Educators and caregivers play a crucial role in this process as well. Teachers, for example, can create a classroom culture that celebrates incremental progress. This can be done through personalized notes, highlighting a child's improvement, or a simple thumbs up when they see a student trying to overcome their fears. In that supportive atmosphere, children are likelier to embrace challenges, knowing they'll be recognized for their efforts.

Peer recognition is also invaluable. Creating opportunities for young people to share their achievements with peers can have a profound impact. Whether it's through team challenges, group projects, or peer mentoring, fostering an environment where peers acknowledge one another reinforces the importance of community support in managing anxiety. By sharing their struggles and successes, children realize they're not alone in their journey.

It's also crucial to involve children in the process of setting goals and evaluating their accomplishments. By having them identify their own achievements, they gain a sense of ownership over their progress. This process might involve setting small, achievable goals that gradually build toward larger milestones. Encouraging them to reflect on what they've accomplished and what they've learned along the way strengthens their self-awareness and confidence in their ability to handle anxiety.

Acknowledging setbacks is just as important as celebrating achievements. When children struggle to meet a goal, recognizing their effort reinforces perseverance and resilience. Discussing these challenges as learning experiences rather than failures promotes a growth mindset. Encouraging this perspective helps children realize that setbacks are not the end but rather an integral part of the journey to overcoming anxiety.

To further support this, caregivers and educators can maintain a log or a journal with the child, documenting each achievement, no matter how small. This tangible record serves as a visual reminder of how far they've come, making progress visible and real. It's a tool that can be revisited during times of doubt, reinforcing the young person's belief in their ability to overcome future challenges.

Ultimately, recognizing and rewarding achievements is about more than just the achievements themselves. It's about inspiring trust in their abilities and instilling a sense of self-worth. When children and adolescents feel valued and understood, they are more motivated to continue working towards managing their anxiety and developing resilience.

As caregivers and supporters, our role in recognizing and rewarding these achievements can't be overstated. By doing so, we not only contribute to their immediate emotional well-being; we lay a foundation for a lifetime of confidence and courage. Let's continue to uplift, inspire, and celebrate the young minds striving to conquer their anxiety one step at a time.

Setting New Goals for Growth

As we close the chapter on celebrating progress, it's important to understand that this is not the end of our journey. Achievements are but milestones on the road to ongoing growth and development. They are meant to be savored and reflected upon, but not as stops where we settle. Progress itself plants the seeds for new aspirations, forging paths to venture further into the terrain of personal growth. Setting new goals is not about merely reaching for the next rung on the ladder but about taking deliberate, introspective steps forward—expanding our horizons both in understanding and capability.

When contemplating the next steps, it's vital to keep the child's interests and strengths in focus. Start by having a heartfelt discussion with your child or adolescent about their experiences, what they found rewarding about reaching their recent goals, and where they felt challenges still linger. It's about listening, really listening, to their views and using these insights as a compass to chart the course ahead. Engaging in this dialogue not only strengthens your relationship but also empowers young people to have a say in their own journey, boosting their confidence and sense of responsibility.

Imagine standing at the observatory of progress, looking back at the trail of achievements and then turning your gaze forward to make out the contours of new ambitions. This practice involves more than just forecasting; it's about crafting a vision that resonates deeply with their own truths. It requires honesty and courage to set goals that challenge yet inspire, that stretch existing capacities while respecting one's current limits. Encourage creativity during this process—sometimes the most unconventional ideas lead to the most rewarding paths. How can their current strengths support these new goals? What surprising capabilities might emerge?

Setting new goals also involves understanding that failure and setbacks are part of the journey. Present these experiences as pivotal learning stages rather than deterrents. Encourage your child to view each obstacle as an opportunity to reassess and adapt their approach. This resilience can be taught through stories and examples, illuminating how others have maneuvered through similar passages of uncertainty and emerged not unscathed but stronger and wiser. By normalizing this aspect of growth, you cultivate a resilient mindset prepared to embrace future challenges with grace.

Once the goals are articulated, the next step is to map out a plan with actionable steps. Break down larger goals into manageable tasks that can be tactically implemented. Celebrate not just the major milestones, but also the smaller victories along the way. Each step, no matter how minute it might seem, contributes to the bigger picture and deserves acknowledgment. This structured yet flexible approach allows for adjustments as interests evolve and new opportunities arise, fostering a dynamic path of growth.

The act of setting goals should reinvigorate and lay a framework for a thriving future. Implement periodic reviews to refocus and realign as necessary, acknowledging progress and recalibrating goals to keep them challenging yet attainable. Flexibility is paramount; the journey is fluid and the route may change, but the destination—the essence of growth—remains steadfast.

Mutual responsibilities are key. Instill an understanding that setting goals is a collaborative effort requiring input and support from family members, caregivers, and mentors. Encourage participation in activities that align with these goals, and when possible, share the adventure by engaging in parallel growth paths. Doing so not only provides a robust support system but also fosters shared experiences and deeper connections.

To solidify these goals and processes, consider documenting them. This can be as formal or informal as desired: creating a vision board, maintaining a goal journal, or even crafting a simple list. Capturing this journey in writing not only clarifies objectives but also acts as a tangible reminder of the commitment made. Over time, these records become cherished artifacts of development, marking where they've been and illuminating pathways to where they are headed.

Goal setting, when intertwined with a sense of celebration and continuous progress, becomes a powerful catalyst for positive change. It nurtures the ability to dream boldly, plan strategically, and act courageously. In the end, the young person doesn't just achieve their goals—they evolve through them, gaining confidence, learning adaptability, and crafting a resilient heart that navigates life's uncertainties with courage and conviction.

As you guide the young ones in your life through setting new goals, remember nothing is insignificant. Every step forward is a promise towards a future filled with possibilities—a future where they grow into confident, independent individuals capable of surpassing the limitations anxiety once imposed upon them.

Chapter 24:
Stories of Courage

Imagine holding a story in your hands that speaks to the very heart of anxiety—tales spun from the yarn of real-life experiences. These narratives aren't just stories; they're powerful testaments to the resilience embedded in the human spirit, particularly in young minds. Take, for instance, Jack, a teenager who discovered his love for painting to express emotions he couldn't quite put into words. Or consider Emma, who turned her fear of public speaking into strength by practicing speeches with her dog as audience—small steps leading to big changes. These stories remind us that the paths to overcoming anxiety are as unique as the individuals who tread them. By learning from others' journeys, young people and their caregivers discover that courage isn't a grand, sweeping act; it's found in moments of vulnerability and the quiet determination to try again. In these shared experiences, we find both inspiration and practical insight, illuminating a pathway through anxiety's shadow, offering hope and fostering the courage to persevere.

Real-Life Experiences

In the vast landscape of childhood and adolescence, anxiety often lurks as an unseen shadow, casting its influence over days that should be filled with wonder and discovery. Yet, for many young individuals, facing this shadow becomes a profound journey of courage and resilience. In this section, we explore real-life stories where anxiety did not define the destination but became a stepping stone toward empowerment and growth.

Take Mia, for instance. Growing up, she felt a constant tightness in her chest whenever she stepped into her bustling high school. The hallways seemed to close in on her, amplifying her fear of not fitting in or failing to achieve the expectations set by her parents. But instead of succumbing to these fears, Mia found solace in art. She transferred her anxiety into vibrant canvases, each stroke of paint a testament to her internal struggles. Over time, art became not only an outlet but a bridge that connected her with others who shared similar experiences. Mia's story is a testament to how creative expression can serve as a lifeline, providing both relief and connection.

Then there's James. His anxiety centered around academic performance, particularly during exams. The pressure to succeed felt overwhelming, and he often experienced paralyzing bouts of doubt and nervousness before tests. James' journey to gaining control over his anxiety began when he was introduced to mindful breathing exercises. At first, the idea seemed almost too simple to be effective. But gradually, as he practiced regularly, James began noticing small changes. The once crippling anxiety began to loosen its grip, and he was able to approach his exams with a clearer mind. James' story is a powerful reminder of how simple mindfulness practices can transform anxious moments into manageable challenges.

Consider the tale of Sarah, whose social anxiety made everyday interactions feel like insurmountable mountains. The mere thought of attending a friend's birthday party would leave her in a cold sweat days in advance. Her path to overcoming this began with taking small steps—starting conversations with classmates she felt most comfortable with and progressively widening her circle. With the support of a dedicated counselor and her family, Sarah learned to challenge her negative thoughts and replace them with positive affirmations. As Sarah's confidence grew, so did her social circle. This personal growth not only reduced her anxiety but also enriched her life in countless ways.

David's story shines a light on how resilience can be cultivated through adversity. Born into a family that frequently moved due to his parents' jobs, David was always the new kid at school. Constant transitions bred uncertainty, fueling his fears of not belonging. Recognizing this pattern, his parents worked with him to develop a coping toolkit that included journaling his feelings and setting small, achievable goals with each move. This proactive approach helped David build adaptive skills and manage his anxiety. Over time, David learned to view change not as a threat but as a series of opportunities for growth and new friendships.

Alex provides another poignant example of courage in the face of anxiety. Struggling with perfectionism, Alex often found himself trapped in a cycle of fear and avoidance. Any mistake seemed catastrophic, and anxiety tightened its grip. It was only after attending therapy sessions that Alex realized the power of self-compassion. Embracing the idea that being imperfect did not equate to failure was transformative. With newfound understanding and empathy for himself, Alex began to embrace challenges and learn from them, turning what once were sources of terror into avenues for personal development.

These narratives, while unique in their details, share a common thread: the realization that anxiety, while intimidating, can be navigated with courage and support. They illustrate the power of personal agency, even in young minds, to transform adversity into growth. Each story offers invaluable insight into the diverse paths that can be taken to confront anxiety, reminding us that there isn't a one-size-fits-all solution but rather a mosaic of strategies and personal breakthroughs.

Parents, caregivers, and young readers can draw inspiration from these real-life experiences, recognizing that they are not alone in their struggles. As these stories unfold, they reveal a map of possibilities, guiding those who feel trapped by anxiety toward a place where confidence and resilience can flourish. Importantly, they highlight the pivotal role of patience, consistency, and unconditional support from family and professionals in this transformative process.

Ultimately, these tales of courage serve as a beacon of hope. They remind us that anxiety, while daunting, is a challenge that can be met with determination and creativity. As we delve into the practical tools and strategies provided in the upcoming chapters, keep in mind these stories of young people who have walked the path of anxiety and emerged stronger, more resilient, and ready to face the world on their terms.

Learning from Others' Journeys

In the rich tapestry of human experience, there are countless stories that shine with the light of courage and resilience. These stories have power. They teach us, inspire us, and perhaps most importantly, they connect us. When navigating the complexities of anxiety, especially for young people and their caregivers, the value of these narratives becomes even more poignant. By learning from others' journeys, we're reminded that we are not alone, and that understanding and conquering anxiety is possible.

Consider the tale of a young girl who struggled with crippling social anxiety. She felt imprisoned by the fear of judgment from her peers. Her journey wasn't easy, but it was marked by small, courageous steps. With the help of a trusted mentor, she practiced speaking in front of a mirror, gradually increasing her comfort level. As she shared her voice—first privately, then publicly—she discovered an unexpected passion for storytelling. Her transformation illustrates that anxiety can be seen not just as an obstacle but as a path leading to personal growth and unexpected discoveries.

Another compelling story is that of a teenager who grappled with severe test anxiety. This young person was exceptionally bright, yet the pressure to perform left him paralyzed with fear. He found solace in cognitive behavioral techniques, learning to reframe his negative thoughts and approach each test with a different mindset. Over time, his grades improved, but more importantly, so did his self-confidence. His journey highlights the impact of mental strategies in altering our perceptions and responses to stress.

We also find strength in the stories shared by parents and caregivers. Take, for example, a mother who navigated her child's anxiety with unwavering patience and creativity. She learned to listen actively, allowing her child to express feelings without fear of judgment. By doing so, she fostered an open and supportive environment, empowering her child to face fears head-on. Her journey teaches us that providing a safe space for young people is crucial in their quest to manage anxiety.

Then, there is the tale of a boy who found that movement and physical activity became his sanctuary. Struggling with anxiety since early childhood, he discovered that sports provided a much-needed outlet. The rhythmic act of running, the camaraderie found in team sports, and the satisfaction of physical exertion offered him a new kind of peace. His story serves as a reminder that sometimes, it's the physical manifestations of anxiety that can be soothed through the body's natural rhythms.

In these stories, and countless others, there is a shared thread of resilience. Each journey is unique, yet they all showcase the remarkable ability of individuals to adapt, to find hope, and to thrive despite challenges. These narratives illuminate the powerful role of community, as those facing anxiety often lean on others—friends, family, mentors—for support and guidance.

Listening to these stories also helps dismantle the stigma surrounding anxiety. When young people and caregivers hear about others who have faced similar struggles, it can lessen feelings of isolation. They begin to see anxiety not as a weakness but as a common human experience that can be managed and overcome. These shared experiences open up dialogues, encourage empathy, and promote a culture of understanding and support.

For a young person facing anxiety, these stories can inspire actionable change. They might be motivated to try new coping mechanisms or to reach out for help. For caregivers, the journeys of others can provide comfort and practical strategies. Learning how someone else successfully managed similar challenges can equip them with new tools and approaches to support their child.

It is also critical to recognize that learning from others does not mean comparing oneself unfavorably. Each individual's journey is different, influenced by a myriad of factors—from personality to environmental influences. The goal is not to mimic each story verbatim but to draw inspiration, to gather ideas, and to foster a mindset open to growth and healing.

Ultimately, stories of courage remind us that anxiety, while daunting, is not insurmountable. They help us build bridges across generations, cultures, and lived experiences, forging communities resilient in the face of adversity. Through these narratives, we can chart a course toward a future where anxiety is not feared but understood and managed, where young people can grow with confidence, and where caregivers feel equipped and empowered to guide and support them.

By cherishing and learning from these journeys, we cultivate a world of empathy and strength, one that emboldens young minds to not only confront their anxiety but to forge paths that are truly their own.

Chapter 25:
Empowering Young Minds

In your journey toward nurturing resilience in young people, one of the most powerful tools at your disposal is the act of empowerment. When children and teens find themselves entangled with anxiety, offering them a sense of autonomy and the agency to face their fears builds their confidence from the inside out. This transformative empowerment doesn't come from shielding them from challenges but instead fostering a supportive environment where they can experience trial and triumph. Encouraging independence in steps allows them to develop problem-solving skills and push past boundaries they once thought insurmountable. The ripple effect of building self-assurance becomes clear when young ones start setting their own goals and embracing both victories and setbacks as part of their unique growth journey. By championing their capabilities and resilience, you help them craft a narrative of strength that lasts a lifetime.

Building Confidence and Independence

Empowering young minds is all about helping children discover who they are, what they're capable of, and how they can navigate the world with confidence and independence. This process begins with creating an environment where children feel safe to explore their abilities and express themselves. Whether it's tackling a fear, learning a new skill, or simply deciding what to wear for school, each decision they make is a building block in their journey towards self-reliance.

One of the keys to building this confidence is allowing children to make choices and take calculated risks. Imagine the power a child feels when they're given the autonomy to decide what activity to pursue or when they can try something new, even if it means stumbling along the way. Parents and caregivers play a crucial role here. By offering a supportive presence but not intervening at every misstep, they show their belief in the child's ability to solve problems on their own.

Independence doesn't mean that children should navigate life's complexities alone. Rather, it's about equipping them with the tools to handle challenges as they arise. Encourage your child to try tasks that they might initially find daunting. Start with small, manageable challenges to help them build a track record of success. Over time, these small victories create a snowball effect that bolsters their self-esteem and resilience.

An essential component of fostering independence is teaching critical thinking and decision-making skills. Consider everyday situations where kids can practice these skills — whether it's planning a family outing or deciding on a hobby. Encourage them to weigh the pros and cons of their choices and reflect on outcomes afterward. This kind of reflective thinking is instrumental in building a sense of responsibility and accountability.

Furthermore, teaching children how to set and achieve goals is another powerful way to instill confidence. Sit down with your child to help them articulate their aspirations and break these down into actionable steps. Achievable goals offer a road map for success and instill a sense of purpose, showing children that they're capable of directing their own lives. Celebrate each achieved goal as it reinforces their sense of competence and achievement.

Encouraging curiosity can also set the stage for confidence and independence. Support their quests for knowledge, whether it's through books, hands-on activities, or exploration. Allow them to ask questions and seek answers, nurturing an independent spirit of learning that will serve them well throughout life. Curiosity leads to discovery, which in turn fuels a child's confidence in their ability to understand the world.

Social situations provide another arena for building confidence. Encourage children to interact with a diverse set of peers and adults. This helps them learn how to navigate different social contexts, understand different perspectives, and manage social anxiety. Role-playing common social scenarios can also prepare them for real-world interactions and reduce anxiety by offering them strategies to handle potential challenges.

Moreover, teaching self-care is an often-overlooked part of fostering independence. When children learn to recognize their own needs — be they emotional, physical, or mental — they begin to understand how to maintain their well-being, even when facing stressors. Show them the value of relaxation techniques, physical exercise, and moments of solitude as means to replenish their energy and sharpen their focus.

Communication is another crucial element in nurturing independence and confidence. When young people feel heard, their self-esteem grows. They're more likely to articulate their thoughts and feelings and ask for help when they truly need it. Make it a habit to set aside time to listen actively to your child, creating a dialogue that underscores mutual respect and understanding.

Lastly, instill a mindset that views challenges as opportunities for growth rather than insurmountable obstacles. It's natural for children to feel discouraged after failures or setbacks. Teach resilience by helping them reframe these moments as chances to learn and improve. This mindset builds a robust foundation for confidence as they come to see that they are strong enough to overcome difficulties.

Building confidence and independence in young minds doesn't happen overnight. It's a gradual process that requires patience, encouragement, and trust. By focusing on these areas, you're not just helping them navigate the challenges of anxiety and uncertainty but also empowering them to thrive now and in the future. Together, these skills will light the path to a more self-assured and resilient life, giving them the freedom to pursue their aspirations and cope with whatever the world throws their way.

Encouraging Lifelong Resilience

Resilience doesn't just happen; it's a quality that we nurture over time in the young people we care about. The journey toward fostering resilience begins with understanding that it's not about avoiding stress or adversity. Instead, it's about developing the capacity to bounce back, perhaps even stronger, from challenges. For parents and caregivers, this journey involves empowering children with the tools and attitudes they need to navigate life's inevitable ups and downs with confidence and grace.

Instilling a Growth Mindset is essential for encouraging resilience. When children believe that their abilities can be developed, they're more likely to embrace challenges and view failures as opportunities for learning. Discussing the stories of famous individuals who overcame significant obstacles can be inspiring and motivational. These narratives shift the perspective from setback to comeback, highlighting the significance of perseverance and effort.

Aside from sharing stories, modeling a growth mindset in everyday situations is critical. Children observe and learn from how adults deal with life's punches. By demonstrating that mistakes are a natural part of learning, caregivers can encourage children to approach problems with curiosity and determination. Simple actions, like acknowledging your own mistakes and discussing what you learned from them, can have a profound impact.

Building Strong Emotional Foundations is another pillar of lifelong resilience. Recognizing and understanding emotions is the first step in being able to manage them effectively. Encourage children to talk about their feelings by creating a safe, open environment where they feel heard and validated. When children can articulate how they feel, they're better able to manage stress and make reasoned decisions.

Creating opportunities for self-reflection and emotional expression, such as through journaling or art, can also support emotional growth. These outlets allow children to explore their emotions safely and constructively, helping them to understand and move through complex feelings.

Strengthening Social Connections plays a crucial role in developing resilience. Encourage kids to form meaningful friendships and participate in community activities. These experiences not only enrich their social lives but also provide vital support networks during difficult times. Having friends to rely on reduces feelings of isolation and builds a sense of belonging, which can buffer against stress.

Parents and caregivers can aid in this process by facilitating social interactions and teaching social skills, such as active listening and empathy. Practicing empathy involves encouraging children to consider different perspectives, fostering a deeper understanding of and connection with others.

It's equally important to allow children the space to solve problems independently. When situations permit, rather than immediately stepping in to resolve conflicts or difficulties, guide young people towards finding their solutions. This practice helps them develop critical problem-solving abilities and boosts their confidence in dealing with future challenges.

Encouraging Self-Efficacy is a vital component of resilience. Children who believe in their capabilities are more likely to persevere when faced with difficulties. To build self-efficacy, set realistic and achievable goals for children, and celebrate their successes, no matter how small. Acknowledging incremental progress reinforces the notion that effort leads to improvement and success.

Resilient children often have a robust sense of control over their lives and are resourceful in seeking ways to handle life's challenges. Encourage them to assess their strengths and weaknesses honestly and to approach setbacks with a plan. Discuss strategies they might use to tackle problems and encourage them to reflect on past situations where they resolved issues successfully.

Cultivating Optimism contributes significantly to lifelong resilience. Teach children to have a positive yet realistic outlook on life. Optimism isn't about ignoring life's difficulties; it's about maintaining hope and believing in positive outcomes. By focusing on what can be done rather than on insurmountable barriers, children learn to view challenges as temporary and manageable.

Incorporate gratitude practices into daily routines to help instill a sense of optimism. Simple activities such as sharing things you are grateful for during meal times can reframe focus onto the positives. This practice can enhance emotional well-being and can provide a greater perspective on life's challenges.

Finally, involve children in *activities that foster physical and mental stamina,* as these are key components of resilience. Regular physical activity isn't just about maintaining health; it's also a great way to relieve stress and boost mood. Engaging in sports or active play with peers can enhance teamwork skills and provide a sense of accomplishment.

Beyond physical activities, involve children in mindfulness practices, such as meditation or yoga, which help in reducing stress and enhancing mental clarity. Teaching them to take a moment to breathe and center themselves when faced with stress can have lasting benefits for emotional regulation and resilience.

In sum, encouraging lifelong resilience in young minds requires an intentional cultivation of a growth mindset, emotional intelligence, social connectedness, self-efficacy, optimism, and physical and mindfulness practices. These elements interwoven into daily life provide children not only with the tools to face adversity but also the confidence to thrive and flourish in an ever-changing world.

Conclusion

As we've journeyed through the intricacies of anxiety and its impact on young minds, it's vital to recognize the unique position you hold as a parent, caregiver, or young person seeking to navigate this complex landscape. This conclusion serves as a call to action and a beacon of hope. It's about realizing the power contained within understanding and managing anxiety, and recognizing it's both an individual and collective journey.

It's essential to remember that anxiety, while challenging, is not insurmountable. The process we've explored together is grounded in fostering a deep understanding and empathy toward the emotional experiences of children and adolescents. Each chapter has shared tools and strategies designed not just for immediate relief but for long-term resilience. This resilience is the armor that equips young minds to face life's uncertainties with courage and adaptability.

By cultivating a supportive environment, we empower young individuals to express their anxieties rather than suppress them. Whether it's through encouraging open conversations or recognizing the thin line between support and enabling, we learn that a secure base is essential. It's crucial, then, to listen actively and validate feelings, allowing room for emotional vulnerability without judgment. When children feel heard and acknowledged, they're more likely to develop trust, not just in others but within themselves.

The journey doesn't end with emotional preparedness alone. Integrating holistic approaches to managing anxiety—like mindfulness, healthy routines, and balanced nutrition—reinforces the mind-body connection. These strategies empower children and teens to self-regulate their emotions effectively. The power lies in small, consistent practices that become second nature over time. When young individuals learn to harness their breath, challenge negative thoughts, and engage in physical activity, they learn that they have agency over their well-being.

Moreover, tackling specific worries, whether social anxiety or academic pressure, requires nuanced strategies tailored to each situation. Teaching gradual exposure and fostering social confidence are pivotal steps. By embracing these challenges rather than avoiding them, young minds can transform fear into mastery. Every small victory propels them toward greater resilience and confidence.

Yet, as much as we focus on the young individuals, it's crucial to address the role of caregivers. Managing your stress and modeling healthy habits is as important as the advice given to your children. Just as in an ecosystem, balance and nurturing are foundational to growth. Self-care is not a luxury but a necessity, allowing you to serve as a stable guide throughout the journey.

Each story of courage, including those shared in this book, serves as a reminder of the strength that lies within every young person. Empowerment is the ultimate goal. This involves not just surviving but thriving despite anxiety. By instilling confidence and encouraging self-expression, you're helping young minds envision a future where challenges are stepping stones to growth, not stumbling blocks.

As we conclude, hold onto the vision of what's possible. A world where children thrive with resilience, creativity, and peace of mind is achievable. It requires a collective commitment to fostering environments of understanding and growth. Celebrate every step of progress, big or small, and continue setting new goals that inspire further development.

As you move forward, continue to engage and evolve with this journey of managing anxiety. Seek out additional resources, whether it's further reading or professional support, to expand your understanding. Know that you're not alone; there's a community of fellow caregivers and professionals dedicated to this cause.

In closing, let this be a reminder that while anxiety is a natural part of being human, it doesn't define or limit potential. Empowerment, resilience, understanding—these are the legacies we can build and pass on to future generations. Let's embrace this journey with hope and determination, knowing that together, we can nurture young minds to not only face the world but to change it for the better.

Appendix A:
Resources and Further Reading

Embarking on the journey to better understand and manage anxiety in children and adolescents can feel daunting. However, with the right resources, you can build a foundation of knowledge and support that's both effective and compassionate. Below is a curated list of books, websites, and organizations that offer invaluable insights and guidance. These resources aim to empower parents, caregivers, and young individuals to tackle anxiety with confidence and resilience.

Books

"The Whole-Brain Child" by Daniel J. Siegel and Tina Payne Bryson - This book offers strategies that highlight children's brain development and how to nurture their mental health.

"The Deepest Well" by Nadine Burke Harris - An exploration of the long-term effects of childhood stress and strategies to combat them.

"Quiet: The Power of Introverts in a World That Can't Stop Talking" by Susan Cain - While not solely about anxiety, this book provides insight into the inner world of introverts, often addressing anxiety as a close relative.

Websites

Child Mind Institute - Offers comprehensive resources and advice for helping children overcome anxiety and other mental health challenges. Visit: www.childmind.org.

Anxiety and Depression Association of America (ADAA) - Provides resources, research, and networking opportunities for those dealing with anxiety and depression. Visit: www.adaa.org.

Mental Health America (MHA) - Offers information and support for a wide range of mental health issues, including anxiety in youth. Visit: www.mhanational.org.

Organizations

National Institute of Mental Health (NIMH) - As a leading federal agency for research on mental disorders, NIMH provides up-to-date information on anxiety disorders and treatments.

The Trevor Project - Supports LGBTQ+ young people with resources and crisis intervention, often addressing anxiety specific to this community.

The Jed Foundation - Focuses on supporting the mental health of teens and young adults, providing resources for reducing anxiety and building resilience.

Delving into these resources can open the pathways to understanding and effectively managing anxiety. Each offers a unique perspective and practical advice that can make a meaningful difference. Remember, continuing education and compassion are the twin pillars of support as you guide young minds through the complex landscapes of anxiety.

www.ingramcontent.com/pod-product-compliance
Lightning Source LLC
Chambersburg PA
CBHW020421290526
45785CB00002B/670